The Little Frog
Awakes

Also by Eline Snel

Breathe Through This

Sitting Still Like a Frog

Sitting Still Like a Frog Activity Book

The Little Frog
Awakes

Mindfulness Exercises
for Toddlers
(and Their Parents)

Eline Snel | Translated by Christiana Hills

Illustrated by Marc Boutavant

SHAMBHALA

Shambhala Publications, Inc.
2129 13th Street
Boulder, Colorado 80302
www.shambhala.com

Originally published in France under the title *L'éveil de la petite grenouille:
La meditation pour les parents avec leurs tout-petits*. © Les Arènes, Paris, 2020;
© Audio script: Eline Snel.

Note: This book should not be regarded as a substitute for competent medical advice.

Cover art: Marc Boutavant
Interior design: Allison Meierding

9 8 7 6 5 4 3 2 1

First U.S. Edition
Printed in the United States of America

⊛ This edition is printed on acid-free paper that meets the
American National Standards Institute Z39.48 Standard.
♻ Shambhala Publications makes every effort to pring on recycled paper.
For more information please visit www.shambhala.com.
Shambhala Publications is distributed worldwide by Penguin Random House, Inc.,
and its subsidiaries.

Library of Congress Cataloging-in-Publication Data
Names: Snel, Eline, author. | Hills, Christiana, translator. | Boutavant,
Marc, illustrator.
Title: The little frog awakes: mindfulness exercises for toddlers (and
their parents) / Eline Snel; translated by Christiana Hills;
illustrated by Marc Boutavant.
Other titles: Éveil de la petite grenouille. English
Description: First U.S. edition. | Boulder, Colorado: Shambhala, [2022] |
Identifiers: LCCN 2021018008 | ISBN 9781611809459 (trade paperback;
acid-free paper)
Subjects: LCSH: Mind and body. | Parent and child. | Child psychology.
Classification: LCC BF161 .S63513 2022 | DDC 128/.2—dc23
LC record available at https://lccn.loc.gov/2021018008

CONTENTS

WHY THIS BOOK?

My children are my teachers. One day, twenty-eight years ago, my youngest daughter, Anne, asked me, "How do you get to sleep?" This question awakened my curiosity. How should I answer such a question? And how can we find good answers to the questions children ask us? At school, for example, Anne's teacher was constantly telling her to calm down or focus, but she never explained how to do it. These were my first steps into looking for solutions in the form of mindfulness and awareness exercises for children, especially as I had already been practicing meditation for a long time. These exercises did a great deal of good for my daughter.

Sometime later, when I was giving a mindfulness course to a group of teachers, one of them said, "It's too bad I didn't learn all this when I was a kid!" That's what led me to develop a method for training children in mindfulness. For several years, the Dutch Ministry of Education has even reimbursed this training method for any teachers who request it.

In 2010, I published my first book, *Sitting Still Like a Frog*, which was translated into English in 2013. I wanted to help parents and children become familiar with mindfulness in a simple, playful way—mindfulness symbolized by a frog. The book teaches them how to be fully present with their minds, hearts, and bodies. I wrote it based on my thirty years of experience teaching meditation and compassion. I felt the need to nourish children's innate sense of curiosity and their natural gifts of empathy and compassion in the face of a society that is becoming more and more demanding. The book was met with huge success all over the world.

In many different countries and cultures, the frog helps children work their attention "muscle"; it tells them what to do so that they can be friends with their emotions. It also teaches them that we don't have to believe all of our thoughts and that kindness is like a soft rain that falls on everybody without forgetting anyone. With the frog, thousands of children ages five and up are practicing their favorite meditations on a daily basis. Not because they are being forced to but because they like doing it. They find calm and feel safe in the middle of life's restlessness and the difficulties that can come with it. The training course for this approach, designed for teachers, psychologists, and parents (the "Eline Snel method") is being used in more and more schools, childcare centers, and private practices.

Over the course of the many workshops and training courses I have given, many participants have asked me if a similar book exists for parents of young children, with advice for managing the stress of getting ready in the morning and prebedtime chaos. How can we find patience and trust in such moments? Where does sadness manifest in the body, and how can we learn to master our anger? In these fast-paced times, it is far from obvious to know how we can wholeheartedly accept our imperfections and identify the things that truly matter in order to live fully. Setting limits on screen time is hard for everyone; it's just as difficult to show yourself kindness and compassion. It's like learning a new language— you have to practice it. And it's up to you to teach all of this to your children.

So, here is the book: *The Little Frog Awakes*, written for children between eighteen months and four years old and their parents, offering awareness exercises for you and your children as well as moments of mindfulness for the whole family.

In this book, children under the age of four will be able to learn through interactive stories, playful awareness exercises, and, above all, your example—the way in which you communicate, the attention you give them, and your presence when they want something they cannot have. The short meditations are ideal for children ages three and up. After age four, children's brains are developed enough to begin practicing the meditations found in *Sitting Still Like a Frog*. At that point, they can learn to name what they feel inside of them, which helps them accept even the most difficult emotions and wildest thoughts and do something with them. It also reinforces positive behavior and sows seeds of self-confidence.

You may find answers to many of your questions, but not all of them. Life doesn't have all the answers; it's too vast, and at times wild and unpredictable. But you can always start by opening yourself up to the richness of the present moment. To *now*. To that smile, that little hand in yours, and your sigh of relief when the kids are finally asleep. All you need to do is truly see your children, listen to them, and understand their whole selves in the present moment, motivated by the deep desire to act in a kind, honest way.

This book explains how you can help your young children become attentive adults, with gentle spirits, warm hearts, and a clear idea of their inner needs, as well as what they can offer the big, wide world around them.

A FEW WORDS ON RAISING YOUNG CHILDREN

We worry a lot about the topic of raising young children. "Am I doing this right?" "Did I react too severely or too half-heartedly?" "Am I too controlling or too lenient?"

You are probably a better parent than you think. You are stronger, but also more vulnerable; crazier, but also braver, and certainly less perfect. It can be calming to realize this. Like every parent, you can also learn to face parental stress, for which some "exercises" could be useful. That is the goal of this book. Because it is simply impossible to steer children into adulthood without some bumps or scratches along the way. We are all shaped by our past hurts and bruises. Ingrained rules, habits, and traditions from our childhood are often reactivated, even amplified at times, as soon as we create our own families. It's not easy to recognize that you're having a power struggle with your strong-willed child if you had a tough upbringing, for example. When you're accustomed to your freedom and a happy, carefree lifestyle, the arrival of a baby can be earth-shattering for you. You need just as much courage to admit that you exclude your partner from the process at times because you think you know far better than they do.

Mindfulness has nothing to do with "good" or "bad." It is an invitation to sit down on a regular basis and stay there. Stop running around in every direction doing something that could be done later. Take the time to let your shoulders fall back down to their natural place, remember how to breathe . . . breathing in this moment of the day . . . and letting go once more. Feel your breath gently enter your chest . . . then your stomach . . . letting your thoughts go free . . . without opposing them, yet without worrying about anything that might happen in the future. It means being fully focused on the moment—that's mindfulness!

Who Is This Book For?

This book is for parents of children between the ages of eighteen months and four years old, and their grandparents and other close caregivers, as well as early childhood professionals, especially preschool teachers and health-care professionals.

This is not a book of recipes or an educational book or a first aid kit. This book is for:

- anyone who wants to learn how to trust themselves— because other people don't always know better than you do;
- anyone who trusts children, because, from the start, they are honest, empathetic, vulnerable, and strong;
- anyone who can be extremely worried but doesn't always let others know;
- anyone who can observe children without prejudice, who avoids giving them labels, such as "She's the musician in the family, and he's as predictable as clockwork";
- anyone who lets children try things they might fail at;
- anyone who, with full attention, wants to listen to children, observe them, and sympathize with them, yet without seeking to analyze, criticize, or urge them on as early as possible (as societal norms tend to dictate).

With this book, and within the context of our society obsessed with success and winning, you will learn how to build a buffer—a buffer against stress, excessive expectations, disappointment, and many of the other challenges involved in raising young children. This book will also teach you how to trust yourself and become convinced that you want to give the best of yourself to the most important person in the world: your child.

1

I WILL NOT BE THAT KIND OF PARENT

....

Perhaps you have already witnessed the following situation at the grocery store: As you wander up and down the aisles, you see a dad pushing a cart with his toddler son sitting in it. The boy is grabbing all kinds of things within his reach and throwing them into the cart. The dad patiently picks each item back up, saying, "No, Sam, we don't need that right now," and puts it back on the shelf. The boy starts crying. The store is being turned upside down. You say to yourself, "I won't be that kind of parent. When my child kicks, screams, or cries because they don't get what they want, I'll discipline them. I'll show them who's boss."

Today, I am that kind of parent. Not at the grocery store but in the car, in the middle of a huge, nearly full parking lot. My two-year-old daughter, who usually loves a little trip out in the car, does not at any cost want me to put on her seat belt. She is squirming and screaming to keep me from buckling her in, and her face is turning red with anger. Some people walking back to their cars look over at us, their eyes full of pity. I feel powerless. I realize I've never really understood what it means to raise a kid who thinks they can do whatever they want. Should I try to talk to her? Sing? Attempt to calm her down? Scold her? Her anger pushes everything away. I can feel my insides starting to boil. I want to disappear.

A family with calm, obedient children approaches us. Their car is right next to mine. The dad glances over at the tangle of arms and legs. I sense a glint of superiority in his gaze. I hate the way this family is looking at us. I don't want anyone, not one person, to look at us. I want my daughter to stop screaming, but instead, she's punching the air all around her. All of a sudden, she escapes from my arms and, with an angry scream, throws her body halfway out of the car. I just manage to grab her by the leg.

How Do You Raise a Child?

Just how do you go about raising a child? Does it require leaving, shouting, hitting? How do you calm down someone who wants to start World War III against you?

I decide to take my daughter out of the car, hold her tight against me, and, first, calm myself down. I take several breaths in, each one a little deeper, and then I start talking to her in a calm, gentle voice. I rock her as I walk. I talk about the colors of the cars around us . . . the blue one, the red one, and the white one . . . and there's another red one . . . and I hum her favorite song . . . again and again. But she isn't defeated. Not yet. She kicks and screams with renewed energy: "Let me go!" And then . . . after walking five times past the red, white, and blue cars, everything changes as suddenly as it began. She sobs for a moment and slowly rests her blond curls on my shoulder. The storm is over—her anger as well. This will certainly not be the first or the last time. But it will always pass. Sometimes, raising a child means simply waiting for the storm to pass. And it always does.

The Toxic Effects of Stress

Every day, we recognize and experience the harmful effects of stress on ourselves and our young families. We have too many things to do. We are on our phones too often and too long, we are restless, we sleep poorly and are chronically fatigued. Our heads are spinning, and there is rarely a blank slot in our schedules. Never before have so many adults and children suffered from burnout.

Now that many scientific studies have shown the damaging effects of stress on both adults and young developing brains, mindfulness is becoming an important topic. With mindfulness, you can give yourself the best. Plus, we know that children are happier when their parents are calm and relaxed.

The Benefits of Mindfulness for Children

A number of studies have shown that mindfulness has a positive influence on important parts of the brain and can promote:

- resilience
- impulse control
- the regulation of emotions
- the ability to change one's mind about things

Mindfulness reinforces self-confidence by helping us discover creative solutions to what may at first appear to be big problems. It supports and stimulates our natural disposition toward gentleness, relationships, friendship, and positive social behavior. More and more scientific studies show that all of these characteristics increase notably in young children who learn mindfulness. Their immature nervous systems and young brains are much more sensitive to the negative effects of stress compared to ours.

Raising children mindfully always starts with you. By practicing mindfulness yourself, you are indirectly giving your child the possibility to become more mindful and access the deepest parts of themselves—the best and most unique parts of who they are. This in turn allows your child to develop these qualities at their own pace, in an open, kind atmosphere. Children learn about mindfulness by imitating you.

Another learning resource comes through the rapid development of language. This means that instead of meditation exercises, this book offers short stories. At this age, it is important for children to play freely and have little conversations about how they feel and what they're thinking at one moment or another. Children don't need a class to learn how to walk. They watch what you do and spontaneously imitate you. There is no better way for them to learn mindfulness, whether in school or at home.

How to Use This Book

This book includes an audio download containing meditations, exercises, and stories.

For parents: There are meditations for every moment of the day. They are designed especially for you. The texts are simple and welcoming so that you can start right away. They are at the core of learning how to be attentive and gentle.

What Is Mindfulness, Anyway?

Mindfulness is simply being present to what is happening now with an open, kind attitude. Being present now, in this moment, without passing judgment, rejecting what is happening—even if it's unpleasant—or letting yourself get swept up in life's distractions and its hustle and bustle. Not by *thinking about* what is happening now but by simply *being* in the here and now.

Practicing mindfulness starts with taking time to stop: stopping our constant flight forward, stopping our habit of worrying about everything and anything. In this way, little by little, the restlessness in our heads and bodies calms down. And we realize we're breathing.

Paying attention to your breath is the heart of meditation. Our breath brings us back to the present moment, to *this* breath. It also helps us notice when our minds wander, distracted by sounds, thoughts about the future, and regrets from the past.

Mindfulness teaches us to be present to our inner world and react in a less automatic way to stress or any difficult situation.

For children: There are stories. But they are much more than just stories. They are exercises to help young children:

- become aware of their breathing (page 22);
- be gentle with themselves and with others (page 92);
- fall asleep (page 118).

You can read these stories to your children yourself or have them listen to them on www.shambhala.com/littlefrogawakesaudio.

For children and parents: There are a few mindfulness exercises that you can do with your children or all together as a family.

Each chapter also presents a few ideas for "moments of mindfulness." They don't require any time—just your attention. Attention for one thing at a time.

Here's how to find them:

The **short meditations for you, the adult,** have this icon:

The **attention activities** have this icon:

The **little stories** for children are on the green pages.

You can find **"moments of mindfulness"** signaled by the words **"Quiet Time"** and this icon:

Remember, practice makes perfect. This is certainly true of mindfulness. By making a regular practice of paying attention to the present moment, not only will you reinforce your attention "muscle" but you will also become more aware of the richness in each and every moment. You will be able to free yourself more often of those automatic remarks such as "Stop!" "No!" "Don't touch that!" When you stop rushing to find answers on the internet or in parenting magazines but rather accept your doubts as normal, you will strengthen your ability to trust yourself. Wisdom is usually found within you rather than outside you.

Training Your Attention Muscle

At the end of this book, there is information on how to download the meditations. They will teach you to press your Stop button and take time to pay attention to what is happening inside you.

Practicing mindfulness is not always straightforward. Habits and thought patterns are not easily broken. The same goes for mental awareness. By practicing the exercises regularly, you will soon become better at noticing when your thoughts start to wander and how you keep dwelling on the past or worrying about the future. Our thoughts never stop. It's their nature. So there's no use trying to stop them. On the other hand, you can stop believing everything they tell you—because most of our thoughts are simply not true!

In Praise of Patience

Mindfulness exercises are not always followed by a result. Just like learning to speak a new language or play a musical instrument, practicing mindfulness requires patience. Until, all of a sudden, you begin to notice small changes in your behavior. Soon you will also notice these changes in your children. A caterpillar doesn't become a butterfly in a day.

With Mindfulness, There's Nothing to Lose

Mindfulness is not about success or failure. It's a way of life, a way of being. It means wanting to be present to pure joy, interrupted sleep, uncontrollable laughter, naughty behavior, and gentle moments. It also means acknowledging when enough is enough, you're at the end of your rope, and you've had it with your children. You don't have to feel ashamed or guilty. You just need to observe and acknowledge what you are experiencing.

Meditating Together or Alone

Meditating together or alone—both are possible. Young children will really love being near you when you meditate, whether sitting in your lap or somewhere near you in the space where you regularly practice meditation. They feel the calm emanating from you. From the age of four or five, they can do meditation themselves (with the help of the book *Sitting Still Like a Frog*). Perhaps you would rather meditate alone. If that is the case, choose a time in your day when it's possible.

"Wisdom is usually found within you rather than outside you."

2

LET'S START AT THE VERY BEGINNING

....

M aybe you've never practiced mindfulness before and you're thinking, "This isn't for me" or "I already have enough things like this to do!" If that is the case, then start out simply, as if you're taking a walk without knowing where you're headed. Just start without any expectations, for a few minutes a day, merely out of curiosity—the curiosity you see every day in your beloved child.

Take the time to observe your inner world from time to time. Observe your thoughts, your emotions, your body. We're not used to stopping to take care of ourselves. We do it for others: our children, our partner, our friends. But we often set aside our own emotions and needs. Or we don't trust them.

A Step Back

To start, all you need to do is to take a step back—sit down calmly, in a place that helps you forget about the outside world. Without closing yourself off to what is happening around you, you can open yourself up to what is living inside of you. Open yourself up and allow yourself to get more and more in touch with someone you're in danger of forgetting: yourself.

Eva, a young mother, is sitting on a bench in her room with her eyes closed. Her hands are relaxed and resting on her knees. She isn't tired—she's meditating for a few minutes while her two-year-old daughter Laura plays on the floor. She does this often, almost every day, when she has the time. Like now.

In a moment, she will do something else.

Right now, there are sounds around her: her breathing . . . a motorcycle going by. There's also her attention. There's no need to react. A finger moves . . . the phone rings . . . There's no rush. Back to her breathing, to the gentle movement of her stomach and her chest.

Laura watches her mother for a moment. She can feel the calm emanating from her. She gets up softly, climbs up onto the bench, and nestles up against her mother. Then she imitates her. Eyes closed, hands on her stomach. They breathe together. And after a little while, Laura falls asleep.

Children Learn by Imitating You

Children learn best by imitating you. They watch how you live, how you play with them, how you look at them. They listen to the words you use for things that aren't allowed or things you see together outside: "Look! A bird, a ladybug, a cow." They can feel if you are present or absent. It doesn't matter whether you're right next to them or in the next room. They watch and listen to how you resolve conflicts and model the same behavior when they play. Try to be calm and soften your voice during arguments. Your example makes them react like you do. You are not only teaching them by telling them what to do but also through your way of being in all those other moments when they need you—the moments of daily life.

"Without closing yourself off to what is happening around you, you can open yourself up to what is living inside of you."

Paying Attention to Your Breath

Mindfulness exercises start with breathing. Paying attention to your breath. Feeling your breath. Not all the time, but at several points throughout the day. As soon as you direct your attention to your breath, as you breathe, you are present in this moment—not thinking about yesterday or stressful situations to come but about right now. And *now* is the moment that matters.

Breathing doesn't change any part of your reality. The goal is not to use breathing to flush away stress, anxiety, sadness, or feelings of rejection. The aim is to behave differently in relation to reality. It's like a note in your pocket when you don't really know what to do next or when you're in danger of drowning in a moment of drama or panic. The message on the note is simple and easy to remember:

- When you're feeling worried or hopeless: *breathe mindfully*.
- When you're angry because you lost your keys and you were very late: *breathe mindfully*.
- When the children have turned everything upside down and you've had it with their fighting: *breathe mindfully*.

Thanks to these moments spent taking several deep, mindful breaths, you can leave your head and enter your body.

Notice that breathing is a singular act. It's a powerful way to connect you to this moment and feel what is happening now, be it calm, worry, or something else. We breathe night and day and find it so normal that we rarely stop. But when you breathe purposefully, your breath becomes an ally, a faithful friend. A friend who doesn't solve your problems for you, who doesn't start by offering advice but who *is* good advice: *breathe* . . . in moments when you feel happy, or hopeless and miserable, and every moment in between.

The little frog becomes a good friend to young children when they are taught very early on in their lives that breathing can be useful when they fall down, when they feel really angry, or when they're afraid of the dark or burglars coming in the night.

Introducing the Little Frog

A frog can teach you how to observe and work on your breathing. It works just as well for your child as it does for you.

A frog has something in common with you and me. It sits. It breathes. And it observes what happens both within and around itself. That's all. It only reacts if necessary. When you watch a frog, you can see its stomach gently rising and falling. That's attention. Attention and breathing. And that is usually all it takes to not be invaded by strong emotions such as fear, anger, joy, or sadness.

Young children really like having a plush frog or a similar frog-related item to go along with the stories and exercises. They can give it a name and talk to it. A plush frog doesn't cost much. You can even make one yourself.

Paying attention to breathing always helps. It works for children, educators, parents, and grandparents alike. It's the first step in reacting mindfully to anything you find stressful, difficult, or heavy.

By feeling and seeing how you react to the various situations you encounter, your child will end up doing the same. I'll say it again—children learn by imitating you. By practicing meditation and reading them the stories about the little frog, together you will familiarize yourselves with the frog's unique form of mindfulness.

The Little Frog Breathes

AGES 3 AND UP

All of the animals have gathered at the edge of the pond for
their birthday party. Since none of them knows how old they
are, the animals have decided that they are all three years old.

Three is a nice number, don't you think?

On the table, there is a big chestnut pie with three candles
and three jars of honey.

A bell rings and the animals all cry, "Happy Birthday!" And
then they all say it again: "Happy Birthday!" They make lots
of noise!

The mouse looks around and asks, "Is everyone here?"
The fox, the caterpillar, the rabbit, the hedgehog, the ladybug,
and the bird repeat her question, shouting, "Is everyone here?"

They make so much noise that they tell themselves that
everyone is probably there.

"No, wait, not everyone is here!" says the mouse. "Where
is the little frog?"

The fox looks at the rabbit, the rabbit looks at the hedgehog,
the hedgehog looks at the caterpillar, the caterpillar looks at
the ladybug . . .

No one knows where the little frog is.

"Wait—look over there!" the mouse says.

They all look over at the other side of the pond, and
there—there's the little frog. The noise isn't bothering her.

She isn't moving.

She is calm. Very, very calm. Her legs are calm, her bottom is calm, and her mouth is silent and closed.

Can you sit calmly like a little frog, too?

So, all the animals gently come over. They can see that one part of the little frog is moving.

"What's that moving, right there, up and down, up and down?"

"That's my breath," the little frog says, "my breath in my tummy."

The breath moves slowly in the frog's little tummy. Her tummy goes up a little . . . and down a little.

Just like you and me.

You can put your hands on your tummy, too . . . right where you feel your tummy moving a little bit.

Can you feel it?

I can feel it, too.

You're doing that so well. You're being calm like a little frog.

Breathing calmly can help you.

It can help when you fall down, when you feel upset or sad, or when you don't want to do something.

Your breath and the little frog are your friends.

Do you want to read about the breath in the frog's little tummy again?

"Goodbye, Little Frog. See you tomorrow."

"Goodbye, (*child's name*)," the little frog says. "See you tomorrow."

Meditation for Parents
Breathing Mindfully

In this audio meditation, you are going to focus on your breathing for ten minutes.

By directing your attention to the movement of your breath, you will simply remain present to this moment . . . Now when you inhale . . . and now when you exhale . . .

At first, you will probably only be able to maintain your focus for a short time before it wanders off again, to thoughts, plans, worries, or other things.

This is how it usually goes—hundreds, thousands of times. Your attention wanders. It's completely normal for everyone.

In mindfulness exercises, it's not about being distracted but noticing that you are distracted. Because you can then bring your attention back to your breath . . . once more . . . *now* . . . This demands courage *and* a conscious choice. The choice, in your perhaps too-full life, is to consciously take the time to stop and sit down for a moment.

To feel yourself breathing.

To feel that you are alive—right now.

Quiet Time

The Golden Fifteen Minutes

Start your day with a golden fifteen minutes! The satisfaction it gives you will last all day. Get up fifteen minutes before your children so that you have time to wake up, find a comfortable position (standing, lying down, or even walking calmly), and become aware of how you're feeling. What do you notice when you pay attention to your body? Where are your thoughts heading?

Give yourself a "gentle start" by calmly and mindfully inhaling and exhaling several times, once more leaving your body at a standstill instead of rushing full speed into the day. Take the time for a short morning meditation.

Morning rituals like this one bring calm and regularity to even the busiest families. The power of repetition makes the simplest everyday moments—such as waking up and getting out of bed—special. And your child will gain something from it, too. They will also learn to wake up calmly. You can agree with your child, even at this young age, that they will remain calmly in bed until their alarm goes off or a little light comes on in their room, and then the day will start with a big morning hug.

And even if it only happens once a week, taking a golden fifteen minutes for yourself can still be a ritual!

3

WHAT REALLY COUNTS

....

Ultimately, when it comes to raising children, there are just four main themes:

1. Attachment
2. Mindful, loving attention
3. Acceptance and authenticity
4. A balance of limits and space

Solid Attachment

When we enter the world, we are vulnerable and entirely dependent on our parents or others taking care of us. When we become parents, we are proud and very happy, but we also feel vulnerable. It happens to us all: in the middle of the night, when a child won't stop crying, we feel overwhelmed. We wish we knew what to do.

It's probably the same for you. Before you had children, you were never in this situation, but you intuitively know and feel what needs to be done. It's new, but it's also ancestral know-how.

What is attachment? It is the deep, vital human need to know we are connected and feel we are understood and loved.

Nourishing, comforting, and loving engagement make up a solid foundation that allows a child to form lasting relationships and learn to face difficulties. That's attachment.

Mindful, Loving Attention

Mindfulness is the natural ability within every human being to be truly present—present to our emotions, thoughts, and what we feel in our bodies. Mindfulness exercises cultivate and strengthen this ability. Mindfulness is like a stabilizer. You could compare it to the keel in a boat that keeps you balanced during intense emotional storms and prevents you from capsizing at the first gust of wind. By learning to mindfully observe your "personal weather conditions," you can return to your own calm in moments of panic, anxiety, or worry. You can also escape being caught up in a storm.

With mindfulness, you experience reality in all its nuances. Mindfulness makes you more open, vulnerable, resilient, and close to others. Children need to learn mindfulness from you in order to recognize it in themselves. By giving words to what you see, hear, and feel, you are teaching your child to always try to better understand themselves and the world around them. Mindfulness requires you to make a choice: you can choose to be mindful. This isn't always easy in a world with all kinds of distractions and a constant stream of digital information demanding our attention. But choosing mindfulness is vital. And you can make that choice *now*.

Acceptance and Authenticity

Acceptance is an inner attitude that consists of acknowledging situations, emotions, thoughts, and behaviors for what they are. This goes for both ourselves and our children, without trying to change or manipulate them and without jumping to conclusions or denial. It means accepting all those moments when your children don't satisfy your expectations, when they don't clean up after themselves, or when you shout at them to stay calm. Acceptance aims to recognize that life is sometimes very upsetting, that you aren't made of steel, and that your children aren't saints.

Authenticity relates to who you are, deep down—your essence. It is a diamond in the rough. It could be polished a little, but it is already completely formed. It will not become much different from what it is now. Acceptance is not the same thing as telling yourself that "everything is okay." On the contrary, it is the profound conviction that you don't need to have thoughts or opinions about your feelings or those of others! Practicing acceptance gives you infinite possibilities to live fully. And to fully love your child, who is so beautifully different from you. Don't be tempted to do everything other people tell you to. Live, love, and have the courage to let yourself be surprised. Life is always different from what we imagine.

Jaw Clenched with Stress

A mother, her hair blowing in the wind, is clutching a young, out-of-control boy in her arms, all while trying to make her way through the crowd with her newborn in a stroller. The little boy hits her face with his fist while he pulls on her hair with his other hand like it's a jungle vine, as if he could use it to swing to freedom. He wants to walk, or run, all over the place. It doesn't matter where. "Let me go! Let me go!"

The mother's jaw is clenched with stress and her eyes are fixed straight in front of her. She pulls a few bunches of hair out of her toddler's hand, picks her fallen glasses up off the ground, and misses an important moment. A moment to get in touch with her own emotion and become aware of her anger.

She closes herself up again. Out of breath and ashamed, she doesn't know what to do anymore. This is exhausting. Of course, she's not the only one who feels this way.

Next time, the little boy will do the same or worse, until there are well-defined rules. Not too many or too few, but just the right amount, not imposed by power but stemming from healthy authority.

Behaviors we deem "unacceptable" demand calm clarification. For this, you need to appeal to your child's innate sense of empathy. But you also need to tell yourself just as clearly how you want this to go: "I don't like when you hit, scream, or hurt others. I want you to stop." When your attitude, contact, and tone of voice are consistent, your child will understand that there is no other option. The message is as clear as day: "Our relationship isn't going to happen in this way."

Limits and Space

Young children do not understand limits. They need rules and regularity, as well as lots of space for discovering what they can already do. They need your reminders to not run in the street, fall into a hole, or get out of bed when their minds are awake but their bodies still want to sleep. If we set limits on their undesirable behavior and give them space for new experiences, they will learn to control their impulses and emotions and not hit something or someone as soon as something doesn't go their way.

Most parents agree about the usefulness of limits. We also agree about maintaining a set of rules and the need for consistency. But this proves more difficult than it first seems. We don't like talking about failure, and we try as hard as possible to prevent tears and arguments. We want our children to be satisfied and happy—preferably always happy and free of danger. In fact, freedom and security, unconditional love, and the possibility to play outside and make messes (except on the couch!) are generally all it takes to help children grow up in a balanced way. But as parents, learning to put up with stubborn demands and not give in right away for fear of being too severe or not gentle enough, takes wisdom and patience. "Please, one more movie." "Well," you think, "that can't be too bad, right? This small victory teaches children, even when they're still little, that whining and insisting five or six times will get them what they want.

Clear rules, applied in a regular, flexible manner ("Today, just this time, you can go to bed a little bit later, because . . ."), bring clarity and peace to the family. Plain language and repeated instructions (the "broken record" technique) yield results. The consequences for certain behaviors must be straightforward, without making punishment necessary. "If you spilled the milk, you can get a cloth to wipe it up." Makes sense, right?

Providing children with limits, but also the space to discover what they already know how to do, shows them the way. Especially when autonomy and the ability to do things "all by myself" are not fully developed. It is better to encourage your child or compliment them than to do things for them. Watch with trust how a toddler fights with difficulty to do something. When they finally succeed, it's fascinating! This is how you sow seeds of self-confidence, thanks to which our children won't give up at the first sign of difficulty and will keep trying until something works.

Seeds of Self-Confidence

Ziggy, age one and a half, wants to walk around the backyard and push her doll in her toy stroller.

The backyard has a fence around it. There are also two steps from the house down into the yard. She wants to go down the two steps with her stroller, but she doesn't know how. She starts to cry. It is a piercing sound. Her parents, sitting in the yard, don't come over to help but instead encourage her: "Come on, Ziggy, give it a try." She takes a little step, then another. She holds the stroller solidly and turns it. She carefully puts a foot on the step and the stroller topples over. The doll falls out. Ziggy puts her back in. It didn't work. Her parents keep calmly encouraging her: "Come on, give it another try, you can do it." She gives her parents a scornful look, then makes a decision. She resolutely grabs the side of the stroller and pushes it down the steps. She sighs with satisfaction. She did it! A seed of self-confidence is sown.

Meditation for Parents

Stopping and Connecting with Yourself

Stopping and Connecting with Yourself is an exercise that can help you pause and learn how to stop. Stop whatever you are doing and become aware of what is happening here, right now. This is an exercise in perception—perceiving your feelings and thoughts; perceiving the way your body is reacting here and the role your breath is playing in it. In this way, you can calmly become aware of your inner state and not forget, ignore, or harass yourself. As often as you can throughout the day, open yourself up to the feelings and thoughts that come to you. You can also try to become aware of what your child is feeling. This will allow you to make a choice: You can choose to react in a kind way, without any expectations or preconceptions. You can choose to react in a mindful, less impulsive way.

A Word about Limits, Screen Time, and Little Brains

Lots of parents wonder about young children and screen time. They also have trouble when their child is glued to their tablet and seems inconsolable if they are prevented from playing with it for even one second. But one second can quickly turn into a long time. Leaving children on tablets for too long, especially on their own, is not without harmful consequences. Excessive screen time disrupts the balanced development of the two sides of the brain and encourages isolation, solitude, and missing out on the key moments in relationships that allow humans to grow: contact, interaction, playing games (outside), and listening to beautiful stories (often the same ones).

Before the age of six (and until the child can read on their own), tablets have no educational benefit. A tablet is like a dog's chewing bone or fake sugar—regular "snacks" of screen time are not good food. They only activate part of the brain and create a subtle dependence on visual and audio stimulation, causing children's brains to crave more and more. This leads them to become agitated and develop the need for sounds to reward them when they press the right button. It's not that they can't do otherwise—they can do otherwise with difficulty. Until you press the Stop button.

Activity

The Stop Button

Most children don't like to be asked to stop an activity they enjoy and want to keep doing for hours, such as playing their favorite game on your smartphone, watching funny videos on YouTube, or simply looking at pictures without knowing what to do with them.

The good news is that we all have a Stop button. Here's how you can present it to a child:

> We all have a Stop button somewhere on our bodies: it might be in the middle of your chest, on your head, on your tummy, in your armpit, or even on your back. Where is your Stop button? As soon as you press it (and only you can press it), it will turn on. And this just means that you stop what you're doing for a moment.

Children really like when you have a Stop button, too. That way they can ask you if you sometimes need to press your Stop button when you've been on your smartphone or laptop for too long, or when you're just lost in thought.

Be a good example at home and put away your smartphone more often. Looking at it together with your child, age two and up, can be fun. But I insist on the word *together*. Because it's important to interact and talk about what's happening.

So, where's your Stop button?

Can you show me where the Stop button is on the little girl?
What about on you?

The "I Don't Want To" Song

I don't want to stop what I'm doing
I really want to keep on playing
If I stop, it'll all be through
One thing's for sure, I'll be blue
And I'll be bored stiff!
I have an idea: How about if
You give me your phone,
And I'll play a bit all on my own?
That way, we can all do what we want!

4

ENTERING OUR INNER WORLDS

....

I see you for the first time.
Your eyes touch my heart.
I look at you more and more,
And I devote my whole heart to you.

have just given birth to my son. I am twenty-five years old and his newborn scent fills the house like a beautiful exotic flower.

He's my first child, and I fell in love at first sight. But imagine my confusion when, from day one, my little love won't stop crying. It's like he thinks I don't know he's there. I'm exhausted and frustrated, and my insecurity builds throughout the day as the noise increases.

On the outside, everything seems comfortable and pleasant. "What a darling!" everyone exclaims. "You're so lucky to have such a beautiful baby." But this does not at all correspond with everything I'm feeling inside, in my inner world. The constant noise often makes me feel hopeless, because it's impossible for me to rest even one moment and because I keep thinking I'm not a good mother. (Otherwise why would he be crying so much?)

I can only start to find my footing in the outside world when I fully open the door to my inner world. My unending exhaustion, my doubts ("Everyone seems to be able to handle this except me!"), and lots of young-mother worries—it all comes out in all its glory. But there is also acknowledgment, allowing acceptance and space for another attitude, even though the situation is more or less the same.

The message is, "Don't expect anything." Be there, attentive to the rocking when you rock your baby, attentive to feeding when you feed him, attentive to changing diapers when you change him. And stop fighting against something that's completely normal, even if it isn't what you want it to be. It's like the midwife's advice: "Bend like a little supple tree in a strong wind."

I was finally able to open myself up to reality: a crying baby, and me, a mother pale with exhaustion on the verge of becoming completely overwhelmed.

I had to accept that the sun was definitely shining on someone else. I'd had a hard labor. I was getting little sleep and constantly worrying about breastfeeding. I felt more anxious than I had ever thought I could be.

I gradually stopped wanting something that wasn't and got myself started with what it was: a baby who cried a lot, until he turned all red, and who needed as much of my attention and love as an angel baby. I fell in love with him all over again and, little by little, I was able to put up with the crying. I rocked him, fed him, and sometimes cried along with him. I walked for hours, pushing him in the stroller, until his crying died down . . . and he could finally sleep. Peace, breath, abandon, relaxation.

In the end, it lasted nine months.

Our inner worlds look like messy barns or caves in which all kinds of things can disappear. "Out of sight, out of mind," we say. Or maybe, "I'll tidy things up another day." By using mindfulness exercises, you look at your inner world with a great deal of kindness and lenience, a calm gaze, and a little distance. As if you're watching a deer standing at the edge of the woods.

Morning Stress: Family Rush Hour

It's still early. Life with two kids is nothing like it was with one. I feel like I've only had two hours of sleep. I went to bed late last night, after several unsuccessful attempts to get my youngest to sleep in her own bed while trying to not wake up the oldest. Full of hope, I turn over in bed. "Mmm . . . this moment is perfect, it feels so nice . . ." When all of a sudden, the feeling is interrupted by the sound of little feet on the stairs. "It can't be . . . No . . . She's never come in this early." As I anxiously keep my eyes closed, with the false hope that the little feet will go just as gently back to their room, our bedroom door opens and my darling daughter climbs up on the bed with the decisive air of an experienced mountain climber all the way up to the summit—me: "I'm awake!"

Everything in my body rebels. I do not want this. *No. Not Now.* I don't want to hear "that," or feel it, or experience it. I want to sleep. For hours, days, maybe even months. But this is now. I feel the weight of everything I don't want building up in my chest. And I sigh a deep, motherly sigh. What was that again about the deer at the edge of the woods?

Acceptance. Making space. For what is, right now. This child's soft body. This moment, early in the morning. Acceptance and refusal: both are there, at the same time.

Responding Instead of Reacting

In the outside world, lots of things hinge on ambition, performance, and comparison, like the images we post on social media to suggest "Everything in my life is fantastic!" In our inner world, there is love. We dream our dreams, and our thoughts are all over the place. It's where all our emotions and expectations live.

As soon as you open yourself up to what's happening in your mind's amazing inner world and you don't react in an impulsive way to what happens to you, you will discover something extremely important. You will learn to know yourself. Right down to the depths of your heart. Who are you? What are you feeling? What's happening inside of you? Responding to a situation means being fully present to your thoughts and emotions, as well as the reactions they provoke, with the goal of learning something from them. And then you can act more mindfully and with more compassion. By regularly taking the time to reflect instead of reacting impulsively, you will contribute to a world of well-being, inner peace, and love for the earth and everything in it. Maybe world peace depends on that.

Meditation for Parents
Facing Parental Stress

All throughout our lives, we find ourselves in stressful situations. It's not unusual to be angry, afraid, sad, or embarrassed. You don't have to avoid these emotions. But you can prevent yourself from being completely overwhelmed by them, continually dwelling on them, or closing yourself off from feeling them at all.

All of our emotions, both the pleasant and the unpleasant ones, make up an important part of human experience. You aren't the only one going through this, even if it sometimes feels that way.

In this exercise, you will learn to feel your emotions for what they are. You will learn to notice them, expose yourself to them, and truly feel them. It's easier if you start by directing your attention to emotions that aren't too strong.

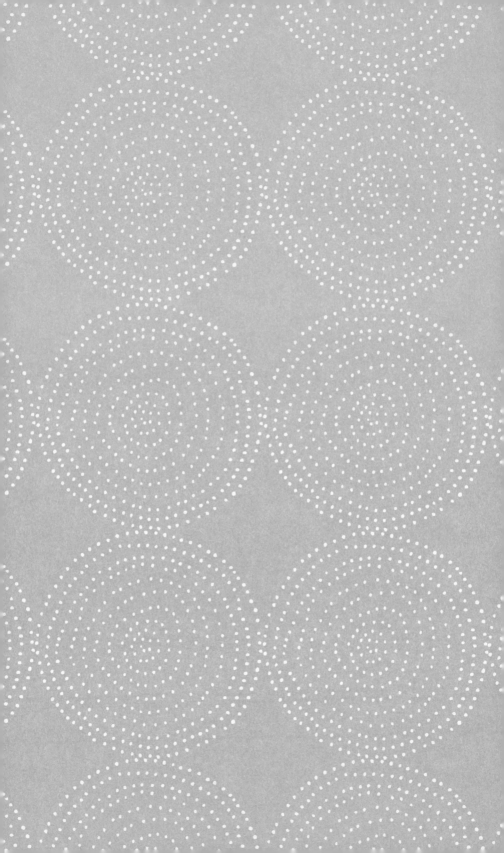

5

YOUR BODY, YOUR FRIEND

....

"I love you, Daddy," says Rebecca, age one and a half, hanging her little chubby arms around her father's neck. Almost unable to breathe, but overwhelmed with love for his daughter, he replies, "I love you, Rebecca . . . so much . . ." and he opens his arms as wide as he can. "More than all the stars in the sky. And more than the sun and the moon put together." Ah! We always have love for our children. The moment they're born, our love is undeniable and indestructible. But what about our love for ourselves? What can we do during the "tough toddler years" so that we're not constantly exhausted or so we don't hit burnout? This season is so intense. Adorable moments quickly follow difficult ones and everything—literally—impacts our bodies in a tangible way.

"I can't remember my body ever being so tired," sighed a mother of twins during the eight-week parenting course. "With two kids, I can't relax at home anymore. And at my part-time job as a general practitioner, I find it harder and harder to focus. I feel like I'm doing nothing but caring for children, washing their hands, and giving them mouthfuls of vegetable purée. But . . . where am I in all this?

Where can I find the time and attention for myself so that I can stay the course?" The other parents in the class can relate. After the last two or three years, no one wakes up well rested anymore. Everyone is under pressure. Life is unpredictable! Even vacations are intense. Other stories follow. Right when it's time for a well-deserved break in a calm, sunny place, your kid vomits all over the whole back seat of the car. Peas go up their nose and won't come back out! Or far more dangerous situations occur, such as a coin disappearing down a baby-who-eats-everything's throat. You can't imagine or predict things like this. But they exhaust you. Especially the little energy suckers who, especially at night, seem to be testing your endurance and patience. These fifteen adults taking the course seem to have an endless supply of stories about excessive fatigue, with just one question: "How can I relax?"

The Listening Test: Listening to Your Body

In fact, we all know the answer to this question. We are all in urgent need of a Pause button. We, too, would love to lie down on the couch with a blanket from time to time while the kids play by themselves. We just want to rest peacefully without doing anything, without our minds being filled with parenting strategies or guilt! Let's put some earplugs in our ears instead of always trying to be attentive to everything.

Then what? Then it's time to start the listening test. Not to test your sense of hearing but to listen to what your body is saying—those signals from your tired shoulders, tender neck, and brain jumbled full of things that would be perfect to do at some point. But you don't need to do anything right now.

Most of the time, we live too much in our heads and not enough in our bodies, even though our bodies can tell us a lot. If you really listen to your body, you will notice the signals it's giving you. Like a fine-tuned instrument, your body reacts to a whole series of emotions, such as anxiety, joy, tension, and exhaustion.

These signals are not there for nothing. They're speaking to you about how you're living right now. They make you feel your limits, along with your need for space and a moment of rest. But we don't always react appropriately. Instead of listening to our bodies, we seek help outside of ourselves. We get a massage or physiotherapy for our tight shoulders. We take pills for pain or lethargy. We have thoughts like, "I don't have time to sit down, because my dear son will wake up the moment I do."

Sometimes we don't trust what we're feeling: "Me, tired? No, everything's fine!" We just keep going. We are brave. And . . . we're in a rush. Rushing to get rid of difficult emotions, we eat chocolate, go on Facebook and Instagram, and scroll through other people's posts that say "Look how happy I am." Whether it's sleeping pills, wine, making ourselves seem excessively happy, or retreating to our phones, none of it really helps.

Mindfulness teaches you to stop for a moment and start to get in touch with your body instead of neglecting it. It will teach you to get back in touch with this part of yourself that is with you wherever you go.

Calm Down

As my son Oliver races on his balance bike across the living room, knocking over a chair and bumping into everything in his path, I often catch myself shouting, "Calm down!"

Saying this phrase helps. Not always for him—but it works for me! This little phrase helps me understand how much I first need to press my Pause button before I can teach my children how to stop whatever they're in the middle of doing. I say it to myself more and more, warmly, like an invitation, a mantra.

"Calm down. Sit down for a moment, get a cup of tea, and relax your shoulders. You're not endangering world peace by stopping for a minute."

Obviously, this isn't possible when the children or the furniture are in danger, but there are many other moments when it is.

As soon as I begin regularly getting in touch with my body, I learn to recognize its gentle signals. I learn to feel it instead of neglecting it or getting worried about it. I calm down more often: when I wake up, when I'm waiting in line at the grocery store . . . or when I'm falling asleep.

It's not always pleasant to be in touch with our bodies. It can even be a source of tension. But it's always a good thing. And it's always beneficial to regularly check whether everything's feeling okay and working properly. When you know this, you can take account of yourself, ask yourself what you need in order to remain in good health and stay as relaxed as possible, so that the little warning lights don't come back on.

Sports and yoga are good ways to, through a certain amount of effort, help you to relax and stay flexible and in shape. Mindfulness exercises make it possible to release physical tension and restore the lost connection with your body. All you need to do is close your eyes and open yourself up to the signals coming from your body. Visit those places where you can feel emotions or tension: in your chest, around your heart, or in your stomach. Collect information without immediately trying to change it or hope for something. Just calm down . . . and things will get better.

Little Bowl Yoga

In this exercise, you will cup your hand like a little bowl and learn to gently tap your body. This will feel really good.

Skin to Skin

If there is one moment in a woman's life when she feels totally present in her body, it's during birth. Fully focused and pushed by her body, she has no choice but to be entirely present.

It got dark very early. The stars are shining brightly in the sky. It's a particularly cold January night when the telephone rings. It's John, my daughter's partner. He asks me if I can come to the hospital. The sweet wait has begun. A deep calm reigns over the soft light of the delivery room. We feel the bond uniting us. The three of us breathe together. Again and again. Unknown natural forces make the body rise and fall. The breathing pauses pass . . . it's time. There is no "later," no "then," just the present pervading everything. Sighs and storms of pain swell and subside. It is high tide. The last wave carries you to me. Two bright eyes look at me. We have never before seen each other like this. Infinitely sweet and pure. It's love at first sight.

Come
Come near . . . nearer still
Contact
Skin to skin
Heart to heart
Connection

"Calm down. Sit for a moment, get a cup of tea, and relax your shoulders. You're not endangering world peace by stopping for a minute."

Meditation for Parents
Taking Care of Your Body

With this meditation, you can give yourself time to get in touch with your body and learn to understand it. We mainly live in our heads, so we don't always notice our bodies' signals or take them into account. In this meditation, you will take the time to simply feel your body, without thinking about it, judging it, or wanting to feel something other than what you're feeling now.

The Magic of Touch

Skin-to-skin contact is vitally important for growing children. It's a primary need, just like eating and sleeping. Children learn first with their bodies. What they experience physically during hugs or light massages with your fingers translates directly into feelings of security, connection, and trust. The skin has receptors that send signals to the brain when it is touched. This contact produces oxytocin, the "cuddle hormone." Touch between children is also important. It teaches them in a natural way how to interact with their own limits and those of others. They develop respect for themselves and others and feel better in their skin. Along with the stimulation of oxytocin, thanks to which we feel loved, skin contact reduces the production of stress hormones. Through playing, tickling, and gentle back scratches, you create a solid foundation for body consciousness, self-confidence, and inner peace. More and more school programs have become attentive to the significance of touch. It's particularly important in our day and age, when children tend to spend too much time sitting and watching a tablet or a parent's phone.

You can never start too early with playful touch and lots of love. The sweet power of touch is healing, nourishing, bonding, and soothing.

Activity

Baby and Toddler Massage

Babies and toddlers really like to be gently massaged while lying on their backs or stomachs.

For Stomachaches or Tension

Massage around the belly button . . . first clockwise . . . then counterclockwise. This natural movement can be done through clothing, about twenty times clockwise and thirty times counterclockwise. You should use about the same amount of pressure as you would to stir soup.

Gentle Back Tickles

At a time of day when your child can relax and rest, take the time to lie them down on the couch on their side or their stomach. Sit down next to them to gently tickle their back and neck for five to ten minutes, making big and small circles. Let your fingers run up and down their back. Your fingers should be as light as a butterfly and move around your child's back without thinking too much about it. Do this in a peaceful setting and enjoy the calm of this moment bonding with your child.

The Art of Touch

Ring Ring (or Ding-Dong)

For children who have trouble eating, start by delicately pulling their earlobe with your thumb and index finger (as if gently pulling a bell) and saying, "Ring ring . . . Who's there?" Next, gently lift one of their eyelids with your index finger, saying, "The little door opens." Then close it, saying, "The little door closes." Then make your finger go up to the top of their nose and slide down, as you say, "We go downstairs, we wipe our feet," (as your finger rubs under their nostrils several times) "and then the mouth opens, and in we go."

I'm Going to Drag You Off to My Lair!

Get a little blanket and let your child roll up in it. Then gently tug the blanket across the floor with your child in it, saying, "I caught you, now I'm going to take you away to my lair! I love little kids . . . Let's go!" You can even make up your own story. This activity gives children the chance to feel the floor with every part of their body.

A Crazy Walk

Most children find it very fun to imitate you when you walk like an elephant or a monster, sneak around like a ninja who no one can see, waddle like a penguin, jump like a frog, or make unexpected twists and turns.

Setting up an obstacle course on the floor is always a success. Your children will learn to coordinate their bodies, correct their balance and attitude, and distinguish between fine and gross motor skills. This can be done outside in your backyard or inside your house.

Quiet Time
Don't Do Anything— Let Things Happen!

When they are older, your children won't really remember your perfectly folded laundry, impeccably ironed clothes, or home-cooked organic meals. On the other hand, they will remember the moments of togetherness and sometimes chaos that prevailed in your home. Moments staying in the kitchen while you cook, or setting the table for dinner, or clearing it afterward.

- Let go of the idea that you must constantly be doing something with them.
- Don't do anything for a moment. Go sit down and purposefully do nothing.
- Take some time for yourself and let your children occupy themselves.
- Don't suggest anything, don't resolve anything; just let yourself be surprised by what happens spontaneously. Good ideas often burst out of nothing.

For the Whole Family: It's Fun to Be Bored!

It's two o'clock in the afternoon. Ruby had a nice little nap, but now she's wide awake. "I have nothing to do. Can I watch a short video on the tablet?" asks my little two-year-old, looking at me. I gently tell her it's not time yet. "When the little alarm goes off, it will be five o'clock and then you can watch a video. Okay?" "Okay," she says, pouting. Then she pulls herself together and says,

"What are we going to do?" I answer, "Nothing, for a little while." "Noth-ing? What's that?" she says, shrugging. "Not doing anything means sitting down for a moment . . . and peacefully looking around you . . . like you're a bird sitting on a branch." Then suddenly I get an idea of something to do. "Hold on. Go sit down for a moment." Right away, Ruby jumps up and says, "You know what I want to do? Some play dough. Can I?"

"Of course, honey, go get it. You know where it is." A few minutes later, she's busy making pink and yellow pies. They are pretty and smell like bubble gum. I suggest, "How about we keep them to surprise Grandpa and Grandma?" "Yeaaah!" she cries happily. And then . . .

As parents, we don't have to be constantly doing something, coming up with great things to do, or making big plans. Children are happy when they have happy parents who aren't always in the middle of something and who aren't always trying to be the best parents in the world. You are more than enough just as you are. Let go of your tendency toward perfection or control. Let your children play their own games and have fun in the background.

6

THE PRESENT MOMENT: A FORGOTTEN NEED

....

When was the last time you stopped for a moment and watched the world within and around you with curiosity, like a child, amazed by what you see, hear, smell, taste, and feel? We've forgotten what it's like. We still know how to do it, but we think we don't have time for it anymore. There are so many other things in our minds: "In a little while, I have to do this" or "Yesterday, it would have been better if I'd said that." We make plans, rush around, and take care of so many things! Our full schedules limit our view of what really has value and meaning.

It doesn't seem so bad to be rushing from one activity to the next without really knowing or sensing where we are. After all, we live in a digital society comparable to a pressure cooker. Walking through the park with your phone in one hand and pushing the stroller with the other, you maneuver around old tree roots that were there before you even came into the world. But you don't see them—there are too many people around and you have to keep moving. Until a child's eyes call you to order.

"Hey! Look!" says my two-year-old granddaughter as we're walking hand in hand toward the grocery store.

"A bode." Surprised, I ask, "What do you see?" "A bode!" she replies somewhat impatiently. "There!" and she points up at the sky. "Ah! Now I see it. A bird . . ." With a few calm beats of its wings, it flies freely through the air. How nice it would be to fly like that. "What else do you see?" "Clouds . . . What about you?" This becomes a nice little game, and an amazingly simple one, as we look around us. Suddenly she lets go of my hand, sits down on the curb, and seems completely absorbed in looking at some object on the ground. I hurriedly cry, "Come on, honey, let's go. The store is about to close. We really don't have time right now." But she does! She has time. Cars and motorcycles whiz by, but she continues to sit and look. "Come look, Grandma." I look at my watch and feel the tension rising in me. Just like my son, she is strong-willed, and I know she won't go into the store until I've looked at whatever wonder she's found there on the asphalt next to the curb. Sighing, I let go of the store. No shopping today. Tomorrow is another day. I lean over next to her. In the middle of the dark-gray asphalt, a little flower is growing up through a crack. Its fragile stem rises up nice and straight, its bud still slightly closed, as if saying, "There's time for everything, don't hurry, come sit down by me . . . and . . . look."

We sit there together on the ground next to the little flower. We look at this fragile life. We are full of admiration. It takes courage to be a flower in the middle of the asphalt with thousands of people walking around you every day. The store is now closed. Hand in hand, we go back home and have toast with jam for dinner.

The Courage of a Flower

It takes courage, the courage of a flower, to remain standing tall in the middle of all the big and little problems that come with the arrival of a baby. From the moment you have a child, your life becomes completely different. Don't be afraid to fail, but try nevertheless to remain sensitive to the details, as if your eyes are right next to your heart, so that you can see that what your child expects from you is the same thing you desperately desired as a child: independence, the opportunity to make your own choices, and love to guide you; the chance to lie in the grass and watch the clouds, to listen to noises, to learn to be aware of your emotions and be able to be very angry without being punished. Everyone has a profound need to be listened to, watched, and understood.

Toast and watching flowers aren't enough to help your children grow. They also need to be able to be themselves and not always have to satisfy expectations that are difficult for them. It's wonderful to not be perfect, and also to never become perfect.

The Art of Observation

Our sensory organs are excellent at observation. They don't judge, and they have no expectations. They live uncensored in the instant present! On the other hand, we have trouble keeping ourselves so open-minded. To sensation, we add mentalization: thoughts and judgments. We are constantly evaluating. We really love having opinions about everything.

Many of us have not reached adulthood without injury. We often surprise ourselves with how we react with more anger, severity, or disappointment than we should or would like to. Those intense emotions that make us panic when our children regularly have tantrums, throwing themselves on the floor, or when they would rather sleep at Grandma's house and not go back home—where do they come from? What about that vague feeling, almost sadness, when your child wants your partner to put them to bed and refuses you? Lots of parents torture themselves and wonder, "What did I do wrong?"

In our unconscious, next to countless happy memories from our childhood, are buried situations that can provoke strong feelings of fragility, anxiety, or helplessness. They float like icebergs in the ocean of repressed infantile affects and an unconscious sense of lack. They generally cause few problems—until the day you have children.

Like Icebergs Drifting in the Ocean

From the moment your children come into the world, unexplored areas, buried emotions, and unspoken needs come to the surface. At the same time, we are suddenly faced with existential questions. Many of us think we will be able to answer most of them. But how? How can we teach a child self-confidence? What can help an inconsolable toddler who can't get to sleep? What do you do when a child is afraid of monsters in their room? Who taught you to "be free" compared to busy grown-ups? Who showed you how to jump in puddles and laugh hysterically about nothing?

Unconsciously, we make decisions that look a lot like what we have experienced in the past. Or we do the complete opposite. Many parents think, "We're going to do things differently; we're going to handle this issue better than our parents did."

During a mindfulness course for parents, we reflect on a series of questions: *What did you love most about your parents when you were a child? And what things do you want to do like they did?*

There is a moment of silence. Memories slowly arise from the shadows of the participants' minds. We tend to hold on to more unpleasant or traumatizing things. "The brain is like Velcro for negative experiences, but Teflon for positive ones. . . . Which is not fair, since probably most of the facts in your life are probably positive or at least neutral," the neuroscientist Rick Hanson explains.[1] This is due to the primitive survival mechanism in the brain stem. Negative events were more threatening, at times with irreversible effects on our survival, so they are carefully stored away in our memories. This is also why it is suggested that it takes five positive interactions to compensate for the effects of a single negative action.

As a result, one young father needs a little time to recall his memories. He finally shares how he used to go on a once-a-year weekend trip with his father. "We brought a backpack and a tent, and we would make a little bonfire in the evenings. It wasn't always fun, like when we had to walk into the wind in a cold rain. But he would always assure me that I could do it. When my children get a little bigger, I want to do the same thing with them. My father is ill now, but we still often talk about our trips: flat tires, a bull near the tent, watching the night sky and making secret wishes on shooting stars. My parents were definitely strict, but in a good way. And . . . they trusted me. Maybe that's what's most important."

Good memories are important. They form a guideline in the forest of opinions about parenting.

But then the course participants are asked another question: *What was missing most in your childhood? And what would you like to do differently with your children?*

The Patience of a Saint, or Survival Strategies

Sophie, a happy mother of three, owns her own business. She is a photographer with lots of clients. Life is good and she has nothing to complain about. Everyone is happy and healthy. Until the day her best friend asks, "Tell me, what do you do to have such infinite patience?"

The never-ending discussions with her daughter Julie about everything and nothing—boots, ham, peanut butter—are exhausting. Bedtime brings more endless talking and questions. Sophie has to ask Julie a hundred times not to interrupt her when she's on the phone. Every three minutes, she has to get up to make sure Julie stays seated at meals. Sophie knowns that her youngest angel holds the power, has little respect for limits, and always has the last word. But she doesn't know how to do things any differently.

Her friend's question falls like a thunderbolt. Sophie tenses up. An image from her childhood suddenly appears. Her mother was strict, often angry, and quickly frustrated. Her father was highly respected and ran a successful communication firm. He was rarely at home and had secret affairs from time to time. Sophie, the oldest of four children, felt responsible. She wanted to help, so she would make sure her brothers and sisters took baths and got dressed, and she often consoled her mother when she was in one of her states again. She was just six years old and she was taking care of her mother like a little mom. She developed long antennae for perceiving others' needs and responding to them. Except her own. Now, the fear of setting limits with her child and of being rejected as soon as she does is amplified. It's an invisible, hidden feeling, but it's undeniable.

Gentle Care for the Soul

During a therapy session with me, Sophie "sees" and "feels" like when she was a little girl: vulnerable, alone, deprived of the affection and conscious attention that every child needs in order to grow. She is more surprised when I ask her what she wants. She isn't used to recognizing her own feelings and needs. But she knows what she always wants to avoid: setting clear limits. It takes compassion to face her old survival habits, to sense who she was before her parents raised her. She needs help to do this work. We have lots of heart-to-heart conversations.

Slowly, something in her changes. She has a decisive moment. The pleasure of parenting gradually replaces the fear of being like her mother. Clear limits take shape. And space—the space to have the right to exist! Together, we make "big boss" and "little boss" posters with photos and illustrated lists of topics that make it clear who is "the boss" of what, without the need for an argument. Julie is the boss of some things, and her mother is the boss of others.

Big Boss and Little Boss

Here's an example. You can discuss with your child how to divvy up what you will each be in charge of. Since your child probably doesn't know how to read, you can add photos or pictures for the different duties.

Julie still presses the Discussion button quite often. But Sophie reacts differently. And that's exactly what makes the difference!

I'm the boss of:

1. Deciding when you wash your face and brush your teeth
2. Deciding when we eat meals
3. Preparing two outfits for you to choose from
4. Putting away toys
5. Deciding how much screen time you have
6. Telling you when it's bedtime
7. _____
8. _____
9. _____
10. _____

I'm the boss of:

1. Washing my face and brushing my teeth by myself
2. Helping set the table and choosing how much I want to eat at meals
3. Choosing one outfit to wear from two options
4. Choosing labels for organizing my toys
5. Choosing what movie or game I want during screen time
6. Choosing a story, a song, or both at bedtime
7. _____
8. _____
9. _____
10. _____

Opening Yourself Up to Rejection

Training your attention muscle gives you the possibility to look at things that hurt you, surprise you, or prevent you from valuing yourself, through a powerful inner lens.

> Felicia, age thirty-eight, has a two-month-old baby and a son who is almost two years old. She enjoys her job, which she works four days a week. She loves her children, but there are times when she wants to cry or wonders if her son loves her. "Ever since my younger son was born, Julian, the oldest, has shown a clear preference for his dad. As soon as Julian rejects me, screaming that he wants his dad and not me to put him to bed, I feel powerless and sad. All kinds of ideas come into my head, like, 'I'm not a good mother because he doesn't want me.' I feel disheartened and insecure. I don't know what to do with these deep feelings of rejection."

This isn't about Felicia or how she is as a mother. It's also not about Julian, or his father being a better parent. It's about how we as parents grasp this kind of situation and the interpretation we often draw from it: "My child doesn't love me, otherwise they wouldn't reject me." We make it personal. Fortunately, conclusions such as this are rarely true—they stem from our childhoods, when we learned this feeling of rejection, sometimes at a very young age. It was often related to our parents, who loved us in their own way but didn't always give us opportunities to talk about what we needed and then try to provide it.

We cannot change these situations, or the thoughts and emotions related to them. However, we can change our *reaction* to them. Your inner attitude determines the weight of your pain.

It's better to open yourself up to emotions than to reject them. It's like paying attention to your best friend. As soon as you do this exercise, a change will occur—not immediately and not every time, but slowly and progressively. And it happens more or less spontaneously, because you are getting in touch with your inner world, feeling out your emotions, carefully going down to those forgotten places of rejection within you, like an archaeologist removing the protective layer of dirt from buried treasures.

Naming, Recognizing, and Accepting

Maybe you are currently very busy, with lots of things demanding your attention and intervention. Maybe you have some things that you just can't stop thinking about and that make you dwell on the way you handled certain situations. What would you say, then, to leaving your head for a moment and focusing your attention on the sensation of your breath?

Quiet Time
Breathing Exercise

Right now, as you're reading, try this: Feel the slight contact of the air as you breathe into your nostrils and then feel the air leaving your nostrils as you breathe out. Continue feeling the life flowing into and out of you . . . at every moment.

Take the time to do this. Once you have, think about a situation that provokes feelings of insecurity, doubt, or a lack of self-confidence in you.

Calmly take the time to discover where in your body you can feel these emotions: in your throat, your heart, your stomach, or somewhere else.

Direct your attention to the part of your body where you can feel these emotions, no matter whether the feeling is mild or intense. What would this feeing look like if you had to draw it?

Come even closer to this feeling . . . and then peacefully say to it: "It's okay, whatever I'm feeling is fine . . . I'm here with you and accept that you exist . . . I'm here with you and I give you my warmest attention, the attention I would give my best friend . . . It's okay . . . I don't need to push you away or turn you into something else . . . but I'm willing and open to learning to recognize you . . . I open myself up to you . . . with curiosity . . . tolerance . . . and calm . . . It's okay."

And then when you've finished, simply return to your breath . . . and feel it right now as you breathe in . . . and out.

Unresolved problems from your childhood can have a disruptive effect on your inner feelings of value, peace, and calm. Of course, you cannot alter what happened in your childhood, but you can change your attitude toward what you are feeling now by moving closer to these emotions instead of running away from them.

Often this is enough. Sometimes, however, additional support in the form of therapy proves necessary.

Without knowing it, children reactivate our zones of pain, sadness, rejection, or lack of autonomy left untreated from childhood. Without realizing it, they trigger the places that provoke strong emotions in us and make us feel we are weak and of no value. That being said, they are also a source of lasting happiness: our children always hold on to us, no matter how they behave or oppose us, simply because we're their parents.

Activity
The Mindful Stroller

Walking gives you energy and allows you to get out of your head and into your body. Walking mindfully takes you a step farther—literally. You can do this exercise with your child in the stroller. Leave whatever you don't need at home (such as your phone, a clear goal, or a shopping list). Just go outside, smell the air, and breathe in freedom. Get your legs moving and walk at a calm pace. Don't do anything else; just walk.

Take in the sights, smells, and sounds of the present moment, feeling each time your feet hit the ground. Do nothing but walk and notice that you're walking. One thing at a time. There's no rush. Just the present, whether you're walking in a bustling city or a wide-open landscape. Walking mindfully is an art in itself. Before you even realize it, thoughts will reappear and you will once more be busy making plans or mulling things over. Decide to do nothing other than walk when you walk. This step . . . and this step. Life is not a race.

Quiet Time

A Mindful Meal

We can all imagine a meal like this, especially at someone else's house: a family calmly seated around the dinner table, everything is tidy, the children are sitting peacefully in their chairs and eating everything, even the stringy green vegetables. But at your house, things are sometimes quite different: in a few seconds, the dinner table looks like a Pollock painting. How is it possible to eat mindfully with young children?

Start at the Beginning

Eating happens at the table, not on the couch. And definitely not walking around with a cup of yogurt. No toys, tablets, or phones on the table—those are put away. Let your child get used to sitting at meals. You should be calmly seated as well. Take time to taste each mouthful. "Mmm, that's good," says my granddaughter, who loves eating. Her brother stops after one mouthful. He doesn't want to eat. He wants to play. His mind is still full of plans, and he gets out of his chair ten times. "I'm going to count to three and on three you need to be back in your chair," his mother says. This takes patience and clarity, but little by little he learns to stay seated while eating.

With Hands or a Spoon?

Toddlers love eating with their hands. Spoons, with their long handles, fall out of little hands at the speed of light. And then there's pasta on their pants and sauce all over the wall. But is it better to let them eat with their hands? Let them do both. Fruits and vegetables, pancakes, and pizza can be eaten with their hands. But yogurt and soup need to be eaten with a bowl and spoon. Before they reach the age of twenty, your children will without a doubt eat with a knife and a fork. It will all work out sometime between now and then.

Is There Still Room in Your Tummy?

When we teach young children to "listen" to their tummies, they can feel when they're full. "Does your tummy want another mouthful, or is it already full?" More and more often, let them choose what you have on the table. But what about vegetables? Three mouthfuls are enough. You can count together. And not wanting to eat them from time to time is also okay. We stay at the dinner table. We can't eat something else. Their appetites will come back, and it's rare for children to not eat when they're hungry. If you do this from a young age, they will learn to pay attention to the food they eat and be in touch with their stomachs. And this is very important in a world where many children are overweight. Toddlers are capable of listening to their "hunger thermometers." It's always good to eat until your stomach tells you it's full.

Rules and a Little Flexibility

Eating mindfully is important, especially at fixed times. This helps you notice when you're full and what tastes delicious, pretty good, or terrible. From time to time, having ice cream before a meal or lots of cookies can make life fun. Sometimes you need to do things you're not normally allowed to do.

Eating mindfully is important!

Activity

What Do You See, What Do You Feel, and What Do You Remember?

It's never too early to work the attention muscle. Here's a simple game that children love.

Get a tray and place a few everyday objects on it (but not too many). Some examples might be a comb, a toy car, a feather, a pincer, a slice of apple, a spoon, and a toy. Cover it all with a dish towel or cloth.

Sit down with your child.

- **Round 1:** Lift the cloth and ask your child to name all of the objects. If your child doesn't know the names for all of them, it can be a chance to learn new words.
- **Round 2:** Cover up the objects and let your child feel each one with their hands: Is it hard or soft? Smooth or rough? Is that the little car? The comb?
- **Round 3:** What disappeared? Take away an object and hide it in your hand. Remove the cloth and ask the child what disappeared. Take away one object each time and see if your child can remember, but without it becoming a competition. It's just a game.

You can also count the objects, or add other variations of your own. The possibilities are endless.

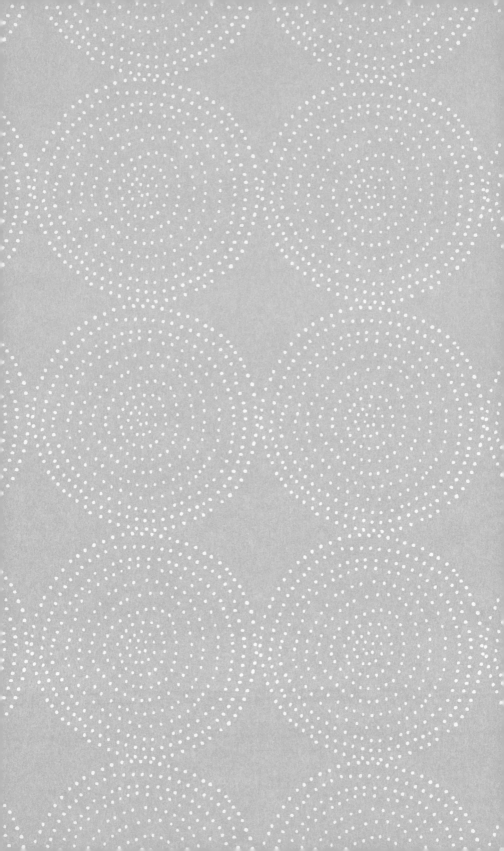

7

THE EMOTIONS
WE FEEL

....

I'm at a doctor's appointment with Tom, my fourteen-month-old son. The time has come for the nurse to measure his height and weight and administer shots. There are lots of people in the office. Tom is calmly sitting in his diaper, already naked on top, waiting his turn. He looks all around him with interest, a scarf hanging carelessly over one shoulder like a Roman emperor. There is so much to see. One child suddenly starts crying, letting out piercing screams. Tom slowly turns his head in the direction of the sound. He seeks contact, feels what the other child is feeling. The look in his eyes is infinitely gentle and tender.

Babies and toddlers do not judge. They don't tell themselves that another child is putting on an act, should stop crying, should be afraid of a shot or not. They know with certainty how to love others. They have the gift of pure, naïve empathy. They naturally feel with others, whether it's you, their grandparents, other children, or nature all around them: "Oh, that bird fell, that's sad. Can we take it home? Can it sleep in my bed?"

Over the course of "the first puberty" (which generally happens between the ages of one and a half and two), their lives suddenly seem a little more complicated. The desire to contradict and the need for autonomy increases: they want to do everything themselves ("On my own!"), except go to bed. A whole series of emotions arise, followed by challenging or regrettable behavior. If you were a little kid, what would you do with your feelings of jealousy and frustration? How do you react when something doesn't work or you don't get what you want? What do you do when you feel unbridled joy or when your sister takes your favorite toy and resolutely declares, "It's mine!"

Space for Emotions and Limits on Behavior

Every emotion is a reaction to something you experience. There are no "good" or "bad" emotions. They are all valid and important. At every age, we need to feel understood, appreciated, and connected to others. These are basic needs. Just like food, water, and a roof over our heads, our emotions bring us security. We always feel our emotions somewhere in our bodies. Our thoughts are in our heads, like little critical voices that have opinions about everything. Especially about what you or your child should feel. Emotions need space; behavior needs limits.

Emotions don't need anything other than your attention—your full attention. Not a solution or well-intentioned analysis. And especially not: "No, you don't have to feel like that." You will connect with your toddler as soon as you accept their emotions and want to understand them. It's as if silken threads tie your hearts together, sending a message each time you connect.

- A YES message: "Yes, I see that you're really mad . . . Or is something making you sad?"
- Or a NO message: "You can't be tired . . . you slept so well last night. I'm the one who's tired—tired of your whining."

A NO Message

"How did today go?" asks the father of four-year-old Clara when he comes to pick her up from day care. "Did you have fun?"

"No," Clara replies. "It wasn't good at all. Stephen hit me."

"Oh, and what did you do?" asks her father.

"Nothing."

"I don't believe you," her father says. "Sometimes you hit, too. I've seen you hit your brother when you're mad at him."

Clara doesn't say a word. She feels sad. Her father doesn't believe her or understand her. He puts her in the car and they drive home. The tone is solemn and the atmosphere has changed. This isn't about Clara's feelings or her behavior. The connecting threads have broken. Without her father's recognition and understanding of her emotions, Clara can't think of a different solution should this kind of situation happen again. She represses her emotions. She closes up like a clam. Her emotions must look for other, less predictable paths in order to express themselves. When the NO message is used too often, children learn very early to no longer trust their own emotions. As a result, they can no longer come up with appropriate solutions on their own to upsetting situations. World peace depends on correcting this!

"Emotions need space; behavior needs limits."

It takes just a few principles for children to learn to trust their emotions:

- Listen to your child attentively and take time to understand what they are saying.
- Imagine yourself feeling your child's emotions.
- Recognize what your child is feeling, look for how it is affecting their body, and help them learn to name their emotions.
- Look for ways to help them work through the emotions. That is how they learn to recognize the different emotions they are feeling and what others are feeling. They learn to name them. Drawing their emotions can help them identify these feelings.

A YES Message

Clara tells her dad more about why she had a bad day because Stephen hit her.

"So, what happened?"

"I wanted the red bike with training wheels, but Stephen wanted it, too. He took the bike from me when I was already sitting on it."

"Oh, I see," her dad says. "And is there only one bike with training wheels?"

Clara nods. She feels understood.

"Then what happened?"

"I wanted to push him, but he hit me. And he left with the bike."

"Do you remember the pictures of the frog?" her dad asks.

fearful

angry

happy

sad

What's the weather for your emotions today?
Can you tell me what the weather is like inside of you?

"Which frog did you feel like inside when Stephen took the bike? The angry frog or the sad frog?"

Clara thinks for a moment.

"Both," she says. "First the angry frog, then the sad frog."

"Yes . . ." her dad says. "It sounds like that's how you felt! Tomorrow, if you want the bike and Stephen wants it too, what are you going to do?"

She pauses again, then says, "I'm going to ask the teacher if we can each have a turn riding it."

"I think that sounds like a good solution," her dad says. And they hold hands and walk into the house together.

The Little Silken Thread

A silken thread is fragile, just like our feelings and our toddlers' feelings. It's not easy to really sense your feelings when you've learned to deny them, ignore them, and not talk about them. This may be one of the most difficult steps: observing your emotions up close and learning to be attentive to how they express themselves. It's not easy to feel and accept emotions that are difficult to contain or quell. But as a parent, you can learn to say YES: "Hmm, yes, I can see that that's making you mad."

We often tend to launch into all kinds of accusations: "He started it, I didn't do anything!" When a child is having an epic tantrum, when they want ice cream or refuse to get a haircut, diversion tactics can be useful; you can say, for example, "Oh, look at that!" or "Hey, there's so-and-so!" But what is the wisest direction to take when your child behaves differently than they have in the past? When they become wilder, quieter, or violent? It won't always be clear to you what's going on within your child. "Difficult" behavior is often related to a "sensitive" emotion.

Hidden emotions are in play, and your child needs loving attention more than evaluation or punishment. They need those little silken threads connecting your hearts to each other, precisely in those moments when you want to cut them.

A Toddler's Buried Pain

Rita teaches preschool. She loves her job, which she has been doing for twenty years, but her class this year is making her life difficult. There are a few unruly kids, especially one named Nicholas, who wreaks havoc in the classroom. This has been going on for several months. Rita doesn't know what's going on with him, but he doesn't listen, he's violent, he messes around a lot, and he can't sit still. She's tried distracting him, putting him in time-out, or giving him a fun activity, but nothing seems to help him calm down. One day, when he gets mad at a boy who accidentally knocked him over, Rita feels sucked into a vortex of exasperation. Suddenly she feels like shouting, "Out in the hallway, now! I've had it!" But precisely at that moment, she feels her powerlessness and her tendency to control with punishment. She takes several deep breaths, each one deeper than the last, makes eye contact with Nicholas, and says in a warm voice, "Nicholas, I can see a thunderstorm has been happening inside you for some time. Is something feeling difficult, or is something making you sad?" Nicholas looks at her in surprise for a moment. The hand he had raised to throw something hangs in the air. Rita made a connection. Someone is truly seeing him. Then his shoulders start to shake. The dam of repressed emotions breaks. He cries for the first time since his little sister got sick.

He can't stop. The other children are as silent as little mice. No one moves or messes around. There is space for his sadness. A few other children start crying when Nicholas talks about what happened to his little sister. She has to go to the hospital every day and sometimes even has to stay overnight. He is left with a babysitter or his grandparents. It's okay, but he misses his daddy and mommy. And he's scared. Scared that his sister won't get better.

Rita listens. She can't offer him a solution, but she can give him her attention. She acknowledges that it can be really sad when your sister is so sick. And it can be difficult if your dad and mom are away a lot and it has to be like that. It's comforting to feel understood. And often, that's enough. Just like now.

Nicholas calms down. In the days and weeks that follow, Rita often asks him how everything's going at home and if he wants to make a drawing of it. Cards with big circles and hearts are taken to the hospital. At home, Nicholas's parents bought him a LEGO set of a hospital. He really applies himself to it, with lots of imagination. Attention works. Always. And his sister, after having a successful operation in another country, is now back home. Life can get back to normal.

Being a Lifeguard

If you teach your children to not reject their feelings, but rather to accept them, they will know how to take their "inner weather" into account and realize that it has an effect on their behavior and on you. When they're in the middle of a tantrum and you are at risk of getting pulled into the whirlwind of emotions, it's not the best time to start discussing what's at stake. What does help is being a lifeguard on a beach.

Squeeze your child tight in your lifesaver arms and take them back to shore. It's only when you're back on solid ground that you can talk about the strong feelings of anger, fear, or sadness churning around inside them. Then you can help them find the right response to their feelings.

Being a lifeguard helps your child—and you—not get trapped in the whirlwind of emotions and disastrous reactions. We can't help what we feel. But we can learn to stop screaming and hitting.

What We Teach Children Lasts

The children in a preschool class are seated in a circle. Bianca, their teacher, has a frog in her lap. It's not a real frog, of course, but a cute, soft, cuddly toy. There are pictures of the frog's four emotions hanging on the wall. The children are talking about their feelings and the places on their bodies where they feel scared, mad, sad, or happy. Each child tells a story and points to the scared, mad, sad, or happy frog. And also how, sometimes, they want to hit, or go hide in a corner, or tell the teacher someone else started it. The children point to the big frog pictures to show where they can feel these emotions in their bodies.

Simon feels anger in his fists. Emma feels sadness in her eyes. "When I'm happy," says Charlotte, "I feel it in my whole body. I'm so happy I feel like dancing and jumping up and down." Martin says he feels scared in his legs and they start shaking. He demonstrates how much they shake—so much that he falls over backward. Then everyone bursts into laughter.

You can teach your children to pay attention to their emotions from the youngest age. You can also talk about how to do it with the gentlest attention—the attention you would give your best friend or your beloved pet. Kicking, pushing, hitting, or throwing doesn't do any good. Emotions are made to be felt, talked about, and shared. And sometimes, we can give someone a hug or say sorry if we hurt them: "I'm sorry I hit you . . . Does it still hurt?"

"Feelings don't last very long," Bianca, the teacher from the above story, tells her class. "They usually appear for just a little while, then they disappear." "But where do they go?" Stephen asks. Is there a place where all our emotions go? What do you think?

"'Difficult' behavior is often related to a 'sensitive' emotion."

Quiet Time | **AGES 3 AND UP**

First Aid for a Stomachache

Interview your stomach (or your head, or wherever you're having a problem).

A lot of children suffer from headaches, abdominal pain, or nausea. They don't understand why, but their stomachs or heads do. For toddlers, being nervous, scared, or having to face something difficult or overly stimulating can often translate into one of these three painful sensations. Of course, sometimes they've just eaten too much, or the pain is caused by something else.

I am sitting with my three-year-old daughter on the couch. A little while ago, after my divorce, she started having stomachaches. When she complains about her stomach again, I ask her, "Where on your tummy does it hurt?" She points to a spot right by her belly button. I ask her to gently rub her tummy with her hands. I tell her to make little circles, then big circles, until she feels her stomach getting nice and soft. "Your stomach knows a lot about stomachaches. Can you ask it why it always hurts? Then listen quietly to what your tummy tells you." After a little pause, I ask her, "So, what is your tummy saying?"

"It says it wants to go to Daddy's house."

"And what about you?"

"I want to go see Daddy, too . . . because I don't like when he's somewhere else."

Then the conversation can begin. Talk about what is difficult, sad, or exciting—and about what can help.

The Little Spot Near the Heart

AGES 3 AND UP

It is a beautiful evening.

The sun is red-hot and the clouds have blown over from the other side of the world.

The frog and the hedgehog are sitting together at the edge of the forest. The hedgehog picks a daisy and asks:

"Frog, do you love me?"

"Of course! I love you very much, Hedgehog. You know that."

The hedgehog sighs.

"Yes, but do you love me all the time?"

"Yes, all the time!" replies the frog.

"Yes, but do you love me when I'm really far away and you can't see me anymore?"

"Yes, even when I can't see you anymore."

— "What about when I'm not nice to you, or when I'm really angry . . . do you still love me then?"

"Of course, I still love you. Whatever you do and wherever you are."

"So, if we really love each other, it's forever and everywhere? Even if we don't see each other every day?"

"Yes," answers the frog. "That's how it always is."

"But," the hedgehog continues, "can I ask you another question? It's the most important question of all: *How do we know we really love someone?*"

Everything grows silent. The forest is calm. Only the trees move gently in the evening breeze.

After a moment, the frog answers:

"You know when you feel it. In a spot near your heart. That's how it always is."

And then they head off into the forest, hand in hand.

They dream about little hearts and love that never disappears.

Even if you don't see each other for a long time.

Meditation for Children | **AGES 3 AND UP**

The Stuffed Animal House

This exercise can stimulate young children's imaginations and their feelings of security and happiness.

Lie down on the couch or the floor with a pillow under your head.

If you'd like, you can close your eyes a little or all the way. I would like to take you to a very special place, a place with a pretty little house. It looks like a dollhouse. Will you come with me? We'll go in together.

The door is already open. And now you are inside. You can see that the entire house is painted in your favorite colors . . . What are they? The sun is shining through the windows. It is nice and warm inside the house. When you go into the bedroom, you see lots of big, soft pillows. You can lie down on them. There are also lots of stuffed animals—a unicorn, a teddy bear, a cow, and a rabbit. What other stuffies are there in the room? Do you see your favorite one?

Now, choose the best place to go lie down, along with your favorite stuffed animal. Set your stuffie on your tummy. It rises and falls gently as your tummy moves. What's making your tummy move like that? Oh yes . . . it's your breath. Feel how your tummy is gently rising and falling right where you're holding your stuffie.

It feels wonderfully calm in your stomach. So calm that your stuffie is almost falling asleep. And so are you. Enjoy this feeling. And when you're ready to start playing again, you can get up calmly.

You can come back to the stuffed animal house anytime you like. It will always be here. It will never disappear.

Activity | **AGES 2 TO 80**

A Little "Pick-Me-Up" for Everyone

Do you ever feel tired? If so, then you can do this exercise. It will give you a boost. It's great to do as a group: parents with their children, grandparents with their grandchildren, or a group of children at school.

For this exercise, stand up with your back nice and straight.

Next, cup your hands like little bowls.

Then bend over and gently start tapping your body. Start with your feet. Keep going until they're fully awake. Now move to your ankles.

Next, with your hands *and* your full attention, tap your shins and calves. Wake them up all the way.

Move up your body and tap your thighs . . . your stomach . . . your back . . . your chest . . .

It's like lots of little frogs with soft feet are jumping all over your body to wake you up . . . Can you feel it?

Then tap the whole length of one arm . . . then the other . . .

Next, wake up your shoulders with some gentle taps and calmly massage the back of your neck.

Now gently touch all the parts of your face with your fingertips . . . then the back and the top of your head . . . like a gentle rain falling on your head and face.

To finish this exercise, calmly massage your child's neck and shoulders and ask them to do the same to you.

Children in a group can sit in a circle all facing the same direction so that each one is behind another child's shoulders to give them a massage.

Waking up your whole body is really pleasant, and so is giving and getting a little massage. Can you feel the difference?

You can do this exercise as often as you like. When you're feeling tired, a bit sluggish, or have a lot on your mind, this exercise gets you out of your head and brings you back into your body.

8

PARENTING ISN'T FOR THE FAINT OF HEART

....

Being a parent is tough. And let's be honest, being parented isn't always pleasant, either. There isn't a universal manual explaining the most effective ways to do things. From the moment you have children, your whole life changes. No one prepared us, much less taught us, to manage all the responsibilities and unexpected situations we face. With barely any time to adjust, but lots of opportunities to learn, one thing quickly becomes clear: life with children is beyond anything we ever imagined!

> We are both with our baby, who is just a few weeks old, at a medical consultation in a big hospital. We "know and feel" that something is wrong, even though all the professionals seem to think that's not the case. We've been told, "It will eventually pass; this happens with most children. I wouldn't worry! Come back in a few weeks if the situation hasn't changed." But of course, we're worried. We've never been so concerned. We're determined to find someone who simply believes us, someone who doesn't keep their distance but who cares about us and says, "If she were my daughter, I'd also want to know what's going on. We're going to keep looking until we find out what it is."

A few days later, we're back in the same office but with a different doctor. She has lots of experience and is a good listener, as much to her patients as to her own gut feelings. Humanity and expertise in the same white coat—what a blessing!

Our baby has to be hospitalized. She is administered a drip, put through a brain scan, and fitted with lots of tubes. The doctor's intuition is faultless: our little girl seems to have a rare brain disease. The coming months are going to be stressful. The insurance claims, too. But nothing will stop us from finding the best pediatrician in the world to help our little girl. Time is of the essence. Through a whole series of detours, we end up tracking down a doctor in another country who is one of the few in the world who has experience with newborn children affected by this disease. We fly over to see him. The operation lasts seven hours. I breathe in love . . . inhaling and exhaling . . . for my child . . . for myself . . . and for the doctor. I breathe in hope . . . for my child . . . for myself . . . and for the doctor. I feel my body, the tension in my stomach . . . the anguish in my heart . . . and I breathe in trust . . . for seven hours . . . waiting . . . breathing . . . there's nothing else to do but wait . . . The operation is a success. Her life can begin afresh, and ours along with hers. We leave the hospital. There is a calm breeze. We breathe deeply and let ourselves enter the world.

What Now?

The world may be perfect in Instagram photos, but everyday reality is different, and that's what we deal with. There is and always will be stress in our lives. There are often more questions than answers to "What now?" There are children who become ill and stay that way. And those who are "different": slower, more distracted. Some have lower levels of cognitive abilities or social behavior. There are children who are afraid of everything and those who are daredevils. And others who live in a world completely different from yours. If that is the case, don't keep your distance—come closer. And stay right there. Trust your intuition and your heart. It's impossible to know in advance what awaits us. The world is both too wild and too forgiving, too promising and too far off the beaten path. But we can patiently learn to trust the change. And learn to let go of the desire to control everything. If we do, we can be free—free to choose the way we manage what's happening within us and in our children's lives.

These skills could be compared to learning to surf. It's not one of the easiest sports, because the ocean waves can't just be stopped or reduced. And you risk falling in the water or panicking. When you learn to surf on the waves of life, you give yourself the possibility to react differently to the difficult meteorological conditions you find yourself in at times. You will have less frustration and fewer mindless reactions. You will have more tenderness and understanding, without losing sight of your limits. You will start to realize that it's not so much the "waves" causing the problems as the way in which you respond to them. That's what makes you free.

When the Unexpected Arises

I asked my son if he wanted to describe his experience when he unexpectedly became a father. When it happened, it was a shock for him. Wasn't it too early? He wrote an open letter to all those who have unexpectedly become parents, who dare to launch themselves lovingly and courageously down the unknown paths of parenthood, who dare to remain curious and perfectly imperfect.

I was twenty-nine years old when I became a father. I felt like it was way too early. A typical case of "not planning on it right now but wanting it to happen at some point." I had the vague idea of starting a family much later, when I would have been a little further along in my career and when the child in me would have matured. In fact, I didn't know what that really meant or when it would happen. Despite the huge waves of love I felt for our newborn son, I struggled to figure out how to combine my "free" life as a musician with my role as a father. What changes would I need to make? Doubts, uncertainties, idealized images of fatherhood, and my ambitions as a composer and musician all fought for priority in my life. Wasn't having a child supposed to be great? The best thing that can happen to a human being? But that's not always how it was. On the days when I took care of the baby, I often had snippets of new songs in my head, their melodies mixing with the invoices I needed to send, while my son wanted to go down the same slide for the hundredth time . . . and then a hundred more. The joys and pains changed as our son grew. It was a pressure cooker of challenges. In three years I went from worrying about his sleep schedule to preoccupations about his socio-emotional development. Little by little, I had to abandon certain expectations. I learned to replace images of what would be ideal with reality. That was one of the most difficult things about parenting: abandoning my expectations and changing what I loved doing so much every day—music! It seemed so contradictory. The mirror that children hold up to you is merciless in the truth it reveals. It's great to seek the best of yourself each day and what still remains to be uncovered, but it demands a lot of energy, discipline, and trust. It's something I didn't always like doing, and I didn't always have the energy it required. My nights are long because of the concerts I do all over the Netherlands. The days are often much too short.

When my son was still very young, I noticed that he was quite different from me. This wasn't surprising, but I realized I had some unconscious idea that my child would be some kind of miniature version of myself. Of course, I knew that each person is born unique. But now I was experiencing it for real. And it had nothing to do with me. For example, whenever I have the time, I like going out to do something, but I noticed that this wasn't a need for him. Was it him? Was it me? Or was I having a hard time "reading" him? I'm an open book, quick to jump into things, always socializing with friends and family. Not him. He's closed up, doesn't talk about his feelings, doesn't make friends easily. When I'm frustrated, impatient, or feel like throwing in the towel, I find a way to go for a run, get out, make music, write a song—those are my passions. I wondered whether this is how it is for all parents, this basic need to flee when nothing's working anymore. Whenever I felt this urgent need, I would disappear to my music studio and start writing about love, leaving, and always being able to come back. I wrote about my father and the fact that it's never too late to tell someone how much you love them.

In the meantime, we had a second child, who is completely the opposite of our first in almost every way. I can see, hear, and feel what's going on inside of him. With the oldest (now nine years old), tests have shown that he is likely somewhere on the autism spectrum. (But who isn't?) Every day, I have to make a "voyage" to his planet. Who are you? What are you thinking? What are you feeling? Please tell me how I can join you. Sometimes I really enjoy doing this, but other times not as much. These "voyages" don't require as much energy to connect with his heart and his mind, which is extremely kind and clever. But none of them ever happens as planned, and I wonder from time to time if it's my fault. Sometimes they are very positive, but not always. So I feel useless, just like so many other parents who feel exactly the same way. Because when I speak with other parents, I realize, fortunately, that I'm not alone. Parenting is not for the faint of heart. It's for parents who dare to surf. Sometimes they fall down even lower than their children, but they get back up and keep going. They live life fully, sing cute songs, and dedicate their hearts to their little ones who don't yet know everything about life.

With my warmest wishes,
Papa Koen, or Diggy Dex[2]

Meditation for Parents

Being Kind to Yourself and Others

We all want to be happy. And we all have the ability to love and feel loved. Without love and tenderness, we risk missing out on opportunities for development and fulfillment. Without love, we are in danger of closing up and isolating ourselves.

You can develop your capacity to love. This doesn't mean that you have to love everyone all the time. It means that you can love as much as possible, in a way that reminds you that this ability is always there and you can always get in touch with it.

Loving yourself is the foundation for loving others. By regularly doing this meditation, you will practice wanting yourself to be happy. Wanting yourself to be happy isn't always easy—we aren't used to it, or we tend to want it for others more often than we do for ourselves.

With the help of this meditation, you will learn to be friends with yourself. It is an unconditional friendship. You will learn to love yourself and continue, with loving attention, to see the good in yourself. This also allows you to continue getting better at seeing the good in others. You can learn to recognize the immense power of love through all the shadows. You can understand it and come back to it as often as possible.

Activity | **AGES 1½ TO 80**

Let's Dance!

Let's dance! Have someone in the family put on music that everyone can dance to. It can be music from Africa or Argentina, salsa or a simple, happy tune. Music allows us to get out of our heads and dive into our bodies. It's wonderful to move around to music with the whole family. And it's surprising to see how your little one starts wiggling around as soon as you start dancing.

Music helps us express our emotions without the need for words. It helps children with their fine and gross motor development and teaches them to recognize rhythms. It also allows them to feel free to move however they feel in the moment.

Quiet Time | **AGES 2 TO 80**

It Takes a Village to Raise a Child

We no longer live in tribes. We no longer wash our laundry together at the river but rather in our own homes with our own washing machines. During the child-rearing years, we often feel alone. A number of studies have shown that children develop better when they grow up in a network larger than the family unit. It's great when your eighty-year-old neighbor comes over for coffee and tells stories about "the good ol' days." Asking mothers and fathers of another nationality to come over for dinner or having dinner in their homes is wonderful as well.

It is also enriching to talk about parenting more often with other parents, so that we can give meaning to our children's lives, to the difficult things and the most enjoyable things. Try to get connected with other parents, not just over the internet but face-to-face, so that you can see their eyes and hear their voice. Share your exhaustion and dare to ask for help from the parents around you. Warmly take the initiative by asking in a considerate manner. Be present. Know how to share your joys and worries. That way, we're not only hanging up our best clothes outside but also our "dirty laundry." This really helps, because you will discover that a lot of parents struggle with the same concerns and questions that you have. Raising children is a tough job. It's not for wimps! Especially in our day and age, when so many people find themselves separated, alone, or burned out.

Take care of one another and one another's children. Help out when someone is facing difficulties alone or suddenly falls ill. Organize weekly pizza nights with friends and neighbors. Parenting with more than just a child's parents is an essential activity—it's a commitment, because you are helping to raise the next generation!

If you fill every waking moment
of your children's lives
they will have no room
to be themselves.
If you push them constantly
they will break.
If you burden them with an abundance
of material toys
their hearts will contract in possessiveness.
If you always try to please them
you will be their prisoner,
not their parent.

— WILLIAM MARTIN, *The Parent's Tao Te Ching:
Ancient Advice for Modern Parents* [3]

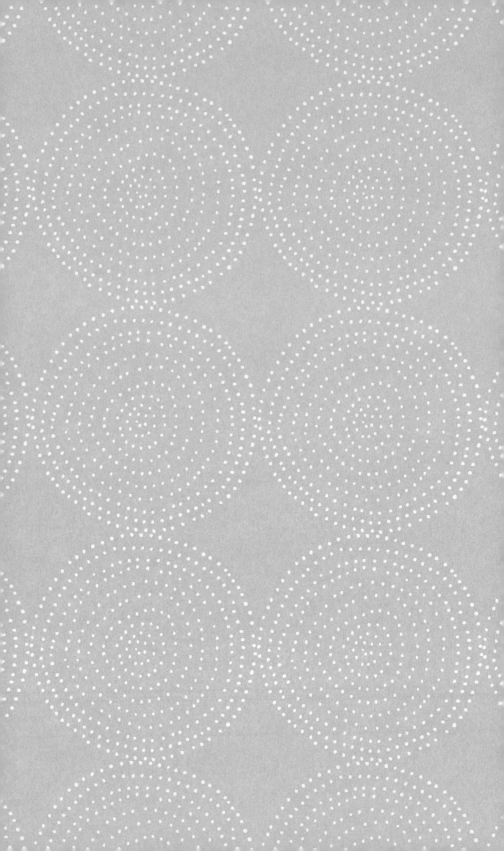

WHEN YOUR BODY WANTS TO SLEEP BUT NOT YOUR HEAD

....

On a regular basis, at the unlikeliest hours of the night, parents find themselves barefoot next to their child's bed rather than cozy and warm in their own. Songs aren't working. Warm milk isn't, either. Even the neighbors are awake. Finally, to stop the chaos, you say, "Okay, fine, you can come sleep in our bed." And that's precisely where sleep problems can begin. Sometimes they don't start with children but rather with your indulgence and exhaustion, and learning inappropriate sleep habits comes as a result. It's not intentional, but we're definitely the ones causing it.

When both parents work and have lots of managerial responsibilities, it's not easy to stick to sleep rituals, get the children in bed, and make them stay there. This is the exact moment when you want to flop down on the couch and do nothing—no fights, no whining. And that's when it starts:

"Julian, are you coming? It's time to go to bed." But Julian, who is almost two years old, immediately says, "No! I want to stay here and watch TV a little longer."

It's already 6:15, and I'm tired. I'm sick of negotiating. I had a long day, and I just want a bit of peace and calm. "Okay, Julian, five more minutes. I'll set the alarm, and when it goes off, I want you to go upstairs without an argument. Okay?" But he's not listening to me anymore. I set the timer for five minutes. The movie's timing is so perfect it would make you jealous. After exactly five minutes, it's over.

We go upstairs, hand in hand. On every step, we have to jump up to the next one: "I want to see if you can do it, Mommy!" "Yes, I can do it, but it's a tiring way to go up the stairs." And if I thought we'd get through brushing teeth without a hitch, I was wrong. My son seems to have an unprecedented number of tricks to make it take forever. He takes everything out of his closet to prevent bedtime from happening. Finally, he's in bed. But now it's 7:00. We read a short story and his eyes slowly close. I'm almost asleep, too. His little nightlight comes on and I make a wish. It would be so nice if just once, bedtime could go smoothly. I whisper, "Sleep well, Julian," as I leave the room on tiptoe.

Learning to Sleep Is Like Learning to Ride a Bike

My prayers have no effect. After ten minutes, I hear, "Mooooooommy . . . I'm scared . . . Can I come into your bed?" I feel like shouting, "I'm scared, too!" Scared of not getting a decent night's sleep, scared of showing up at work on autopilot with bags under my eyes. But instead, I call up to him that I'm coming. I've just started taking a parenting course. This is the first night. I go back upstairs. I sit down in the chair in his room . . . and, little by little, I start applying the "Learning to Sleep Is Like Learning to Ride a Bike" method.

Night 1: Calm before Bedtime and a Clear Bedtime Ritual

A good start is already half the work. Setting definitive times for taking a bath, brushing teeth, putting on pajamas, and getting into bed must not be flexible or delayed. I made up my mind. There was no more room for discussion, but there was space for saying goodbye to the day: Sleep well, teddy bear. Good night, lamps. Farewell, bright moon. To end the day, I rock him for a few minutes, holding him in my arms like a baby. He asks, "Hmm, one more time?" Just one more time. His body relaxes. He's tired. Then it's time for a lullaby and a little story. Julian picks a book from a choice of three. Then the lamp goes out and the little nightlight comes on. I sit down next to him, relax, and say that I'll stay right next to him until he falls asleep. He can't leave his bed. I breathe in . . . I stand guard . . . I help him feel secure. "It's dark, Mommy. Can you turn the lamp back on? I'm scared." I mumble a "Hmm" and say something to the effect of all children are sleeping now so that they can play tomorrow. He closes his eyes again. "Mommy, I hear something." I mutter another "Hmm . . . I'm right here, honey, just close your eyes . . . Nothing can happen to you." "Mommy, do goldfish close their eyes when they sleep, too?" Me: "Hmm." I give him his pacifier, place my hand on his head for a moment, come up close to his teddy, and simply say, "Sleep well, Julian. I'll stay right here with you a little longer until you fall asleep . . . Close your eyes." This takes half an hour, then he falls asleep. He wakes up a few times that night, cries, and wants to come into our bed. I go back to him, reassure him, and wait with him for a little while until he goes back to sleep—in his own bed.

Night 2: Rest, Regularity, and Staying in Bed

The ritual is not changed or delayed. This is made clear to Julian. My presence is meant to be reassuring. Due to the clear succession of one activity following the next, there's no room for a never-ending conversation. The little story is read, the animal friends are cuddled, the lamp is turned off, the nightlight comes on. I sit down a little farther away from his bed, slightly out of his field of vision. I hear his need for attention—"One more story" or "I'm thirsty"—but I don't react. It's hard to unlearn an ingrained habit. It's hard for a child to learn to sleep in their own bed when their parents always give in to their crying and whining by saying, "Okay, fine, come on." But I've made up my mind. I leave his room with the meditation: "Sleep well." I go downstairs, leaving his door open. Twenty minutes later, I can hear him crying from time to time, calling for me, and I really want to go back up, but I realize that in order to learn to ride a bike, sometimes you have to leave a child so that they feel that they can do it themselves. I stay near his room and distract myself with a few things that need to be done.

Night 3: "In Two Minutes, I'll Come Back One More Time"

Now, our bedtime ritual works on its own. Julian knows the order of activities and no longer argues when it's time to go to bed. After a story and a short conversation about our day, I set into motion the meditation: "Sleep well," and I peacefully leave his room. I stay nearby. After three minutes, I peek back into his room. He is sound asleep.

In two weeks, Julian learned to go to sleep. He learned to fall asleep independently, like learning to ride a bike. First, on a little seat in front of me. Then, on a bike with training wheels. He knows how to do it! He knows how to do it all by himself!

From time to time he still wakes up in the middle of the night because something scares him. A gentle touch on the head and his little nightlight are usually enough.

No child is like any other. Sometimes something in the bedtime ritual needs to be changed because you become better and better at sensing what your child needs. Some hyperactive children need a very strict ritual with no exceptions or arguments. With calmer children, you can allow a little variation. And if sleep remains a problem, you may consider consulting a medical professional to see whether there could be a physiological issue.

Many studies have shown that one in four children under the age of five suffers from a sleep problem. I've received hundreds of emails from parents telling me how their children can now fall asleep during the "Sleep well" meditation. Has your child already discovered the secret of the little sleeping animal? John, age two, asks to hear the story on page 118 each evening and sometimes falls asleep before it is over. He discovered the secret.

The Secret of the Little Sleeping Animal

AGES 2 AND UP

In a hut at the top of a tree lives a little animal.

There are lots of other animals in the forest, but because this animal is little and always wants to sleep, he is called the Little Sleeping Animal.

It's almost evening. The stars and the moon are finding their places in the sky. The sun is going down, little by little. *Poof!* All of a sudden, it disappears.

The forest becomes quiet, very quiet . . .

Soon, all of the animals go to sleep. The Little Sleeping Animal yawns . . . A very big yawn . . . "Ahhhhh!" But he's not asleep yet. He's writing a letter . . . a secret letter . . .

"Whooo is that letter for?" the owl asks.

"Oh, it's a letter for all the children of the world," says the Little Sleeping Animal.

"All the children of the world?" the owl says. "What are you writing to all the children of the world?"

The Little Sleeping Animal can hardly keep his eyes open. He answers with a big yawn, "Ahhhhh . . . I'm telling them that to sleep, you always start by yawning . . . and that . . . Ahhhhh . . . Ohhhhh . . . I'm so sleepy . . . I can barely manage to stay awake . . ."

He gently rubs his eyes and yawns again a few more times: "Ahhhhh! Ahhhhh!"

Here comes the hedgehog. Just like the owl, he can't sleep at night. He asks, "So? What happens after all those yawns?"

"Ahhhhh!" yawns the Little Sleeping Animal. And he yawns once more: "Ahhhhh!"

And—*poof!*—there he goes! After a very long yawn, the Little Sleeping Animal falls into a deep, deep sleep . . .

He dreams about little children yawning . . . and sleeping well. He dreams of little children yawning . . . He dreams about his toys, his favorite games, and his friends, the animals of the forest. And the secret to sleeping well . . .

Shhhhhh . . . it's nighttime . . .

Sleep well . . .

Meditation for Children | **AGES 2–3 AND UP**

Fall Asleep

Sleeping is a very particular thing: Sometimes, children have played a lot and they are tired. Sometimes, they don't feel like sleeping at all. Or perhaps, like my daughter used to say, their bodies are tired but not their minds.

Here's a short meditation to help them get to sleep. It may be useful for them to first listen to "The Secret of the Little Sleeping Animal," then this short meditation. Or simply one of the two. It works very well.

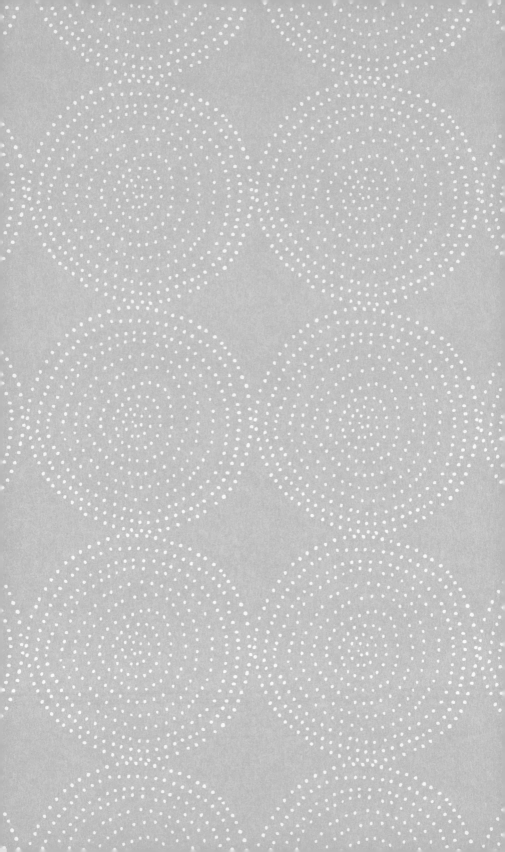

10

THE GARDEN OF SOULS

....

What do you want to be?
the teacher asked.
I was in third grade.
I looked at her
without knowing what to say.
I thought I was already something.
— TOON HERMANS [4]

You Have Less Influence Than You Think

Raising children is hard work. Everyone in a child's world exerts
an influence on their development. As a parent, you want the best
for your children, but there are a number of circumstances you
cannot control. A child's development is the result of their skills,
how they are raised, and a lot of chance experiences.

If you relativize the fact that you are not responsible for your
children's "failure" or "success," you will be more relaxed and stop
feeling guilty about things that may have gone poorly. Then they
will have more space to grow and grow until they reach adulthood—which they will, no matter what happens. Children may
not always listen to you the most, but they are experts in copying
your behavior.

Children Are Their Own People

Children are their own people. Perhaps even the most curious people on the planet. They come into the world with an inner garden, their very own unique "soul garden" in which there are already all kinds of things they have built and achieved. Their garden may be quite different from your own, with colorful flowers, strange bushes, and well-rooted shrubs that you may never have seen before. And, like in every garden, there are also weeds growing here and there.

By observing your child's inner garden with curiosity, surprise, and an open mind, you will discover everything there is to be found there: tenderness and strength, still water or raging rapids. When the trunks are solid, the characteristics are clearly visible. Young branches show flexibility and vigorous growth. Authority, anger, social skills, kindness, impatience, or difficulty connecting are all rooted in a child's inner makeup.

What would your child's soul garden look like if you had to draw it? What about your own? What paths connect your two gardens? By carefully maintaining these spaces, you can see what needs to be pruned from time to time because one side is growing too much and you need to make more space for the sun. By learning to recognize yourself as a "gardener," you will discover where you like to go and where you don't like to go. What parts of the garden do you find difficult to maintain, and what help would you like with them?

A parent's task is not to change the makeup of their child's garden or to plant their own plants and flowers there. You don't need to transform your child's garden. You just need to give it enough light, water, and love, along with the trust that it will grow and flourish on its own. Attention and love make every garden and every gardener pleasant and happy.

Kind Acceptance of Imperfection

As a parent, you are probably very familiar with the vague feeling of not doing well, and it comes back on a regular basis. Those doubts about yourself intensify when you see someone else's garden, which always looks greener than yours: the neighbor across the street who always comes up with the best stories; the super-parents who only do responsible things and play intelligent games with their children, and who are always coherent—"Your children don't eat vegetables? Mine eat everything and go to bed without a fuss. It's so amazing to only have to say things once."

It's not easy to dare to be vulnerable and allow your children to be as well. Not having to do everything well is a blessing, a relief at a time when society expects so much of us and we expect so much of ourselves. Too often we compare ourselves with others and judge ourselves based on standards of "what should be." It's not easy to feel that what we're doing is not enough or that we're not being kind—or not kind enough.

Having children doesn't mean always being happy. It's often difficult and sometimes a real shock. Forget everything you think you know about those amazing moms and extremely considerate dads. Live your life, love, and trust your heart and your own good sense. Take the time to stop for a moment and simply observe what's happening right in front of your eyes. And laugh at all those imperatives you force on yourself: "That's okay, it doesn't have to be perfect. I don't have to be the best." We all have our uncertainties. Stop for a moment. Take the time to observe and understand what's happening inside of you. Everything starts there—and there's no end! Only now!

You don't have to make your children happy.
They already are, simply because you're there with
them.
I wish you good luck.
And lots of success with the meditation exercises
and the stories.
I wish for your children and you to be even more
attentive to this world.
I wish for your children to trust you and for you
to fully benefit from what is.

ACKNOWLEDGMENTS

Every day, I have hundreds of reasons to be thankful, but I want to name those whom I wish to thank in particular for their warm involvement in the process of writing and publishing this work.

First and foremost, my children and grandchildren, who are an inexhaustible source of inspiration. Equal thanks goes to my husband, Henk, who reads everything I write and comments on it with his gentle wisdom, teaching experience, and researcher's eye. He is with me in my thoughts at every moment. He always gives me the freedom to hide away for months in my office to write. Even during our vacations. Anytime, day or night, I can make him a part of my ideas. Without him, this book would not exist.

I am very grateful to all the parents and children whom I've met over the years, whether in the street, at the grocery store, or during the countless mindfulness courses I have taught. Their questions, stories, and experiences inspired me to write this book and enjoy doing so.

I also want to thank the friends of the amazing team of teachers and administrative staff of the Academy for Mindful Teaching: Peggy Carlier, Mark Hansen, Astrid Hollander, and Ingrid Kroeze. They begged me to write until I found the time to keep writing. They read the stories from this book to their children and gave me precise suggestions. You all are the best!

My friend Yolanda Derksen, who works in a children's day care, is a faithful reader of my manuscripts. She would always say with a sigh, "If only I had had this book when my children were little!"

I want to thank Jacques Van Rillaer, a professor emeritus in psychology, from the bottom of my heart for his beautiful translations of my books into French. No one else could have so sensitively translated the language of children and my playful expressions like he did.

I want to thank Julia Foldenyi, from Shared Stories Rights Agency, for her enthusiasm and meticulous communication with both me and publishers around the world and for getting my books published in over thirty-eight countries.

This brings me to Les Arènes, my favorite French publisher, which is ahead of everyone else. They pour their hearts into the books they publish. New ideas come together in marvelous ways. I have never seen such professionalism, creativity, bravery, and love for authors and their works in such a fabulous team!

I want to especially thank Catherine Meyer for her tireless aid, enthusiasm, and friendship. Along with Marc Boutavant, the incomparable illustrator whose talent has given the frog and his friends their unique look, such that children around the world can welcome them into their hearts. For children, the frog has become a symbol of loving attention for themselves and others. Thank you to the entire Arènes team for their renewed confidence.

Finally, thank you to my readers and their children. "Sitting still like a frog" has become an oft-used expression, thanks to their attention, and is now widespread in the practice of mindfulness in families and schools.

Inspiring Books for Parents

Faber, Adele, and Elaine Mazlich. *How to Talk So Kids Will Listen and Listen So Kids Will Talk.* New York: Scribner, 2012.

Faber, Joanna, and Julie King. *How to Talk So Little Kids Will Listen.* New York: Simon & Schuster, 2017.

Kabat-Zinn, Myla, and Jon Kabat-Zinn. *Everyday Blessings: Mindfulness for Parents.* New York: Little, Brown, 2014.

Neff, Kristin. *Self-Compassion: The Proven Power of Being Kind to Yourself.* New York: William Morrow, 2011.

Siegel, Daniel J., and Tina Payne Bryson. *No-Drama Discipline.* New York: Bantam, 2014.

———. *The Whole-Brain Child: 12 Revolutionary Strategies to Nurture Your Child's Developing Mind.* New York: Bantam, 2012.

———. *The Yes Brain: How to Cultivate Courage, Curiosity, and Resilience in Your Child.* New York: Bantam, 2018.

♫

AUDIO DOWNLOADS

You can download the meditations and stories to listen to on a smartphone or tablet. In order to download the audio, visit www.shambhala.com/littlefrogawakesaudio.

NOTES

1. Rick Hanson, *Just One Thing: Developing a Buddha Brain One Simple Practice at a Time* (Oakland, CA: New Harbinger Publications, 2011), 17.
2. Diggy Dex is a rapper, singer, and songwriter from the Netherlands.
3. William Martin, *The Parent's Tao Te Ching: Ancient Advice for Modern Parents* (New York: Marlowe, 1999), 17.
4. Dutch humorist, singer, and poet.

Eline Snel (b. 1954), Founder and Director of the Academy for Mindful Teaching

Alongside my practice as a therapist, over forty years ago (in 1980), I started developing and teaching a course in mindfulness and meditation for adults. I am curious, attentive, open, and searching for the essence of things, and I have never been focused on results. Rather, I am interested in well-being and how to be present with full attention.

In 2004, several school directors asked me if I could develop a mindfulness method for children. At the time, such a thing didn't exist and no one had written on the subject. Yet it seemed much needed everywhere, in every culture. This request brought about a period of deep personal transformation in me. With the soul of a child in my mind's eye, I developed the Eline Snel Mindfulness Method for children (ages four and up) and adolescents (ages twelve to twenty-one).

The challenge was to create a training course for professionals that didn't just focus on the brain and a goal but that was rooted in ancestral wisdom and compassion, combined with new perspectives, neuroscience, and many years of experience. This course had to not only provide a method for teaching mindfulness to children but also give a central role to personal experience with meditation and compassion and allow the best in each instructor to blossom. The Academy for Mindful Teaching (AMT) was founded in 2008. Now, over twelve years later, it is considered one of the best institutes for teaching mindfulness to children, teachers, and parents—the perfect trio. The method is scientifically validated and has proven useful in teaching environments.

Our training team, administrative office, and online store do not simply guarantee the quality of our content and personalized involvement: we are what we do! And perhaps that makes the difference.

Besides the three manuals I have written for education professionals, I also have developed mobile applications (also suitable for parents of young children), which is available for Android and iPhone in several languages (Sitting Still, as well as a program for kids in the Mind app), an activity book for children (*Sitting Still Like a Frog Activity Book*), and The Flying Frog, a game for Air France. I also created a mindfulness periodical designed for people following an eight-week training course.

For parents and education professionals, I wrote *Sitting Still Like a Frog*, which has sold over a million copies around the world, and *Breathe Through This*.

To learn more about the training courses and workshops we offer in a number of countries, visit www.elinesnel.com.